Successful Bra...
Management
In A Week

Paul Hitchens and Julia Hitchens

WITHDRAWN

The Teach Yourself series has been trusted around the world
for over 60 years. This series of 'In A Week' business books is
designed to help people at all levels and around the world to
further their careers. Learn in a week what the experts learn in
a lifetime.

Paul Hitchens and Julia Hitchens have over 40 years' combined experience in the creative industries, working in advertising, branding, design and marketing. They are the husband and wife team behind Verve Brand Consultancy.

Since 1996 Paul and Julia have helped hundreds of businesses to realize their brand's potential through consultancy, seminars and training workshops. Their brand name 'Verve' means 'energy, enthusiasm and dynamism', all values required for brand building.

Paul and Julia are co-authors of *Create the Perfect Brand*, a Teach Yourself guide to branding. Together they have also written and presented a series of brand training workshops for executive education. Their specialist courses include Brand Identity, Brand Touchpoints and Employer Branding. Paul Hitchens is a Course Director for the Chartered Institute of Marketing and presents the CIM Branding Masterclass.

For more information about Verve Brand Consultancy, visit: www.verve.co.uk

Dedicated to our sons Guy and Miles

With thanks to our parents Howard and Sheila Dowding, John and Catherine Hitchens

Successful Brand Management

Paul Hitchens and
Julia Hitchens

www.inaweek.co.uk

First published in Great Britain in 2014 by Hodder & Stoughton. An Hachette UK company.

First published in US in 2014 by The McGraw-Hill Companies, Inc.

British Library Cataloguing in Publication Data: a catalogue record for this title is available from the British Library.

Library of Congress Catalog Card Number: on file.

10 9 8 7 6 5 4 3 2 1

The publisher has used its best endeavours to ensure that any website addresses referred to in this book are correct and active at the time of going to press. However, the publisher and the author have no responsibility for the websites and can make no guarantee that a site will remain live or that the content will remain relevant, decent or appropriate.

The publisher has made every effort to mark as such all words which it believes to be trademarks. The publisher should also like to make it clear that the presence of a word in the book, whether marked or unmarked, in no way affects its legal status as a trademark.

Every reasonable effort has been made by the publisher to trace the copyright holders of material in this book. Any errors or omissions should be notified in writing to the publisher, who will endeavour to rectify the situation for any reprints and future editions.

Typeset by Cenveo® Publisher Services.

Printed and bound in Great Britain by CPI Group (UK) Ltd, Croydon CRO 4YY.

Hodder & Stoughton policy is to use papers that are natural, renewable and recyclable products and made from wood grown in sustainable forests. The logging and manufacturing processes are expected to conform to the environmental regulations of the country of origin.

Hodder & Stoughton Ltd

338 Euston Road

London NW1 3BH

www.hodder.co.uk

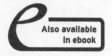

Contents

Introduction

What's your favourite brand?

This question reveals so much about us because brands are the things we care about, the things we aspire to and the things we identify ourselves with. Brands are the football club you follow, the watch you promised yourself and the pair of shoes that says you've arrived.

The name Apple consistently tops the popularity league when people are asked to name their favourite brand. At Steve Jobs' Commencement Address at Stanford University in 2005 he said, 'Have the courage to follow your heart and intuition. They somehow already know what you truly want to become. Everything else is secondary.' The late founder of Apple was speaking to an audience of graduates but his words offer great advice to every entrepreneur and individual starting on a voyage to build a brand today. His honesty and candour highlight the importance of integrity and authenticity, now prerequisite in an era of transparency.

Building a strong brand takes much more than a week: it takes a never-ending commitment to excellence. This book provides a seven-day insight into the principles of brand management. It takes you from the conceptual stage through to planning and all the way to implementation. It's packed with tips and insights to help you jump-start your brand and give you the tools and confidence to manage it through the hurdles of the business landscape.

Successful brands are like famous personalities – they have ways of doing things that we instantly recognize and expect. They have a distinctive look, feel and tone of voice that we associate with them. If you consider your brand as a living personality, you will find it easier to bring it to life and have meaning. Managing a successful brand is about knowing the brand thoroughly so that you can instinctively guide it through the stages of growth to provide a consistent experience to its audience. The Walt Disney Company has an Institute dedicated to best practices in leadership, culture, customer experience, brand loyalty, creativity and innovation. The success of a brand is largely due to employees who share a commitment to the brand's ethos and ideals and who are empowered to act intuitively to deliver the brand promise. As the employees or 'cast members' at Disney would say, 'What would Walt do?'

Apple's iconic 'Think different' advertising campaign was created by TBWA/Chiat/Day in 2007 and ran as both television and print advertisements. The campaign featured famous global thought leaders from the past and present. Its words are inspirational and could apply to anyone considering building a new brand:

'Here's to the crazy ones. The rebels. The troublemakers. The ones who see things differently. While some may see them as the crazy ones, we see genius. Because the people who are crazy enough to think they can change the world are the ones who do.'

We wish you every success with your brand!

For more information and social media links, please visit www.verve.co.uk

Paul Hitchens, MCIM Chartered Marketer
Julia Hitchens, DipM MCIM Chartered Marketer

SUNDAY

Determine your brand focus

It all starts with an idea, a seed of hope that must germinate, flourish and blossom if it is to grow into a successful brand. It has to be a big, bold idea to branch out and attract the attention of its intended audience in a patchwork landscape of competing brands. The big concept challenges the status quo, ignores boundaries and excites the imagination. Big ideas change the game and upset the old order.

Big ideas often start with a bold question: how can we make the world a better place? Contrary to popular belief, all the best ideas have not already been taken. There will always be room for another good one. The best ideas are simple and easy to comprehend and can be shared and transmitted effortlessly to the right audience.

Some of the world's biggest brands are based on simple ideas, beautifully executed. When a brand stands for something, it creates meaning for the product, service or organization. A brand comes to fruition through a manifesto, a clear declaration of intent, supported by promises and aims and underwritten with a core belief.

What's your big idea?

SUNDAY
MONDAY
TUESDAY
WEDNESDAY
THURSDAY
FRIDAY
SATURDAY

Brand definition

If you spoke to a hundred people and asked them to define what a **brand** is, the chances are you would get a hundred different answers and that's because brands are many things to many people. Some of the most popular brand definitions include personality, promise, trust, experience and love. Brands come in all shapes and sizes including organization brands, product and service brands and the term may also be extended to describe people and places. The 'brand' word has become extremely popular and is in danger of overuse, but it serves an important purpose to describe all those attributes – emotional, physical, mental and soulful – that we associate with a particular experience.

The perception of brands is based on their past (reputation), present (experience) and future (expectation).

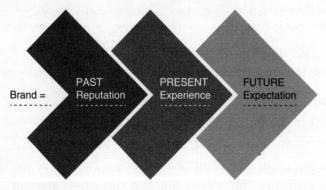

Brand perception

- **Reputation:** A good reputation is earned by delivery of the brand promise with a consistent service that builds trust and brand equity.
- **Experience:** Successful brands deliver uniquely satisfying experiences that create emotional and psychological bonds of loyalty.
- **Expectation:** Through reputation and experience, consumers interpret meaning in their favourite brands. When a brand stands for something, it is expected to behave in accordance with its character.

TIP *There is a popular misconception that a logo is a brand. The logo is not the brand; it is a signpost to the brand experience. Together with the associated brand identity elements – the name, strapline, colour, typeface and aesthetics – the logo serves to authenticate and identify the legitimate brand.*

Brand history

Brands have been guiding choice for centuries, pre-dating the Industrial Revolution. Museums are filled with archaeological artefacts demonstrating the proud work of craftsmen from ancient civilizations who left their mark on valuables including implements, pottery, coins, jewellery and objects of veneration. Branding – the need to proclaim your name and mark your territory – is part of the human condition.

The first use of the word 'brand' in a business context was related to the practice of using hot irons to burn indelible symbolic markings into the hides of cattle for the purpose of identification en route to market. Today, brands aim to leave indelible marks in our consciousness, maintaining them in our thoughts.

The Industrial Revolution and the subsequent boom in factories saw the need to differentiate manufactured goods from competing businesses, through the use of attractive packaging and persuasive advertising carrying the legend of the brand. Some of the most familiar brands today can boast long histories of satisfied customers: think of Moët & Chandon (1743), Birkenstock (1774), Cadbury (1824) and Levi Strauss (1873).

Why do I need a brand?

The reasons for creating a brand or rebranding an existing organization, product or service are many and varied. These are a few examples:

● to launch a new organization, product or service
● for the relaunch of an existing organization, product or service
● in rebuilding a lost reputation

SATURDAY FRIDAY THURSDAY WEDNESDAY TUESDAY MONDAY SUNDAY

- to unite or consolidate a group
- new ownership
- new positioning
- to attract and retain staff
- to attract investors
- to attract customers.

It's impossible to avoid creating a brand; people will make up their mind about you one way or another and, once that opinion is made, it can be very hard to change. This is why it is imperative to create an intentional brand and not one that is left to chance.

There are major benefits to be gained from creating a brand, including the following:

- **Differentiation:** Branding makes it clear to the consumer why a product is better than any other on offer.
- **Connecting with people:** Brands connect with people, culturally, economically and emotionally. A strong brand will earn customer loyalty.
- **Added value:** Brands create value by adding an emotional significance that exceeds the basic value of the product or service.
- **Signify change:** Branding makes business strategy visible. This could be a change of ownership, change of direction or change of market, or the launch of a new product or a start-up business.

Brand valuation

Building a successful brand is a prudent investment for the future that makes a significant contribution to the overall value of an enterprise. Brands are classed as 'intangible assets', a term which covers all forms of knowledge that contribute to an organization, such as reputation, skills and knowledge, employees, customer and supplier relationships, goodwill, contracts, domain names, software and processes. Brands are different from 'tangible assets', which have a physical presence and include factories, machinery and equipment, for example. A brand is a valuable business asset, but few businesses have any idea what that asset is worth.

The financial community values brands for financial reporting, planning mergers and acquisitions, and tax compliance. Marketers need brand values for brand portfolio management, setting budgets and gauging performance.

Establishing a brand's value is necessary for:

- brand investment decisions
- marketing budget allocation
- communication of brand worth
- the balance sheet (when acquiring a brand)
- mergers and acquisitions
- securing finance.

ISO 10668

ISO 10668 is the world's first brand valuation standard and was released in 2010. It specifies the procedures and methods for monetary brand value measurement that are required to provide financial evidence of the brand's worth. The standard provides a stable method for valuing any brand. The brand valuator must undertake three types of analysis before passing judgement on the value of the brand: legal, behavioural and financial. This three-stage approach may be applied to new brands, brand extensions and existing brands.

These are the three stages involved in ISO 10668 brand valuation:

1 **Legal analysis:** Define what is meant by 'brand' including trademarks and intellectual property rights.
2 **Behavioural analysis:** Predicted stakeholder behaviour for geographical, customer and product areas where the brand is operational.
3 **Financial analysis:** The ISO standard stipulates three valuation methods: market, cost and income. The nature of the brand will dictate the appropriate method.
   - **The market approach** measures the value of the brand based on what other purchasers in the market have paid for similar assets.
   - **The cost approach** measures the value of the brand based on the cost invested in it.

- **The income approach** measures the future income that the brand may generate and the costs of generating that income over the economic life of the brand.

Brand valuation reports

Brand Finance, Interbrand and Millward Brown are three consultancies that publish high-profile annual reports on global brand valuation based on their own methodologies. Brand valuations can produce widely differing values and may be viewed as an art form rather than a science. The true value of the brand can only be realized when the brand is sold – or, as the godfather of branding Wally Olins wrote in *Marketing Week* (August 2011), 'A brand is worth only what you are prepared to pay for it.'

Brand architecture

Brand architecture makes business strategy visible through the hierarchical management of brands. Through the lifetime of any business enterprise a number of scenarios are likely to affect its structure: first, new products and services may be launched; secondly, business acquisitions are accumulated; and thirdly, corporate mergers are a possibility. Brand architecture is a strategic tool that communicates the structure of the organization and how the branded assets in its portfolio relate to each other and their respective audience(s).

Brand architecture applies logic and coherence across a portfolio of products and services to differentiate and connect with audiences. A managed portfolio creates greater impact, market clarity and organizational synergy, increasing the brand's value. The consequences of an incoherent brand structure lead to audience confusion, market weakness and operational inefficiencies.

Models

There are three broad brand architecture models – single, endorsed and branded – and there are many variations within and overlaps between these categories.

Single brand model

This model may also be referred to as 'monolithic', 'master brand' or a 'branded house'.

The single brand model applies a solitary approach to brand identity and positioning across every aspect of the enterprise and its operations. Nearly every new business venture begins with the single brand model.

This strategy is the easiest to manage because each facet of the organization supports a single idea and this makes it very clear to the audience what is being offered. It is an economical approach to implement and build brand value through repeated exposure and accumulated recognition. The drawback with this approach is that one crisis can lead to a loss of reputation throughout the entire operation.

Single brand model example: **Virgin** – Virgin Atlantic, Virgin Trains, Virgin Media, etc.

Endorsed brand model

The endorsed brand model presents a portfolio of independent brands, each endorsed by the organizational parent brand. This model is suited to acquisition and allows the endorser to retain the loyalty and recognition of the acquired brand's customers while placing it under the security of its group name. The parent brand gives credibility and maintains its profile for the benefit of the shareholder.

This is a popular model in the food sector where household brand names can be bought and sold between larger conglomerates.

Endorsed brand model example: **Nestlé** – Nestlé Shreddies, Nestlé Cheerios, Nestlé Milkybar, Nestlé Kit Kat, etc.

Branded model

This model may also be referred to as a 'house of brands'.

The branded model is a portfolio of brands each with its own brand identity and positioning. The parent company typically keeps a low profile so as not to confuse the message of the individual brands. The branded model allows the parent company to compete at different value points in the same sector without harming consumer perception. If the brand is managed carefully, it can be traded between holding companies with its identity and positioning intact without damaging consumer perception.

The drawback with this model is that consumers are demanding transparency, and a sophisticated audience will want to know who is behind the brand. Extreme scenarios of this model may be criticized as a covert way of creating a market monopoly.

Branded model example: **Swatch** – Swatch, Tissot, Longines, Omega, Breguet, etc.

Sub-brands

Sub-brands are a portfolio of products or services that are linked to the parent brand. The sub-brand borrows equity from the parent brand and leverages value from its relationship. The product or service typically has its own name but is closely associated with a family resemblance between parent and siblings.

Sub-brand model example: **Dell** – Ultrabook, XPS, Inspiron and Alienware.

Brand planning

Before you can write a winning brand strategy, you need a big idea. It could be an exciting new product, a much-needed new service or a new kind of organization. Whatever the idea, it is important to establish from the beginning who will be responsible for what.

It is absolutely essential that the management team and key decision-makers in an established organization are involved from the start: business owner, founder, Chief Executive, Managing Director and heads of finance, marketing, sales, human resources (HR) and key stakeholder groups. This is not a job for the marketing team to undertake in isolation; it requires total buy-in from the top table from the beginning. This is because everything is at stake – the new brand will need to be at the strategic heart of every future initiative if it is to succeed.

Research

If you are going to undertake the rebranding of an existing business, it is recommended that you arrange a tour of the organization to gain an insight into the everyday running of the business. It is important to take a deep interest in the operation and its products and services at every level in order to get a good feel for the environment, atmosphere and culture.

It will help to make a collection of all existing marketing collateral for the brand from past and present.

> **TIP** *A video diary capturing popular public opinion can help provide further insights and you might consider interviewing the public about their thoughts on this type of company, product or service, for example.*

Research to consider

- **Marketing collateral for the organization and its competitors:** stationery, forms, publications, advertising, press releases, newspaper coverage, trade press coverage, packaging, sales literature, website, blog, Twitter, social media exposure, exhibitions, uniform, badges, merchandise, etc.
- **Human resources collateral for the organization's employees:** induction material, recruitment campaigns, internal communication information, history, structure and management hierarchy, etc.
- **Research reports:** trends, statistics, surveys, reports from industry, trade associations and local and central government.

Key stakeholders' workshop

It is an important part of the formulation of a brand strategy to conduct an initial workshop or series of fact-finding interviews with key stakeholders. This should include the management team, major shareholders and a representative viewpoint from employee and customer groups.

The interviewer or workshop presenter must be intuitive and sensitive in order to pick up important information because it is often the things that are left unspoken that can be the most illuminating. This information will be helpful in formulating the brand strategy and creating the brand identity.

The research questions

The following questions are helpful in provoking honest answers about the nascent brand. What you are looking for is a gut reaction to your questions, without prior warning of what will be asked.

- What is your marketplace like?
- What are your competitors like?
- Describe a typical customer.
- How do you make the world a better place?
- What is it like to work for your organization?
- Express your business vision for five years' time.
- What would you avoid or include when describing your company?
- Describe your business in a single sentence.

At the research stage it helps to get a raw intuitive perspective of the brand idea.

Brand archetypes and storytelling

Every big brand idea needs to be shared if it is to gain traction (i.e. popularity and acceptance). The original, most effective way of sharing information is the ancient art of storytelling. The best stories are engaging; they strike a chord and stimulate emotions. Soap operas and TV dramas are populated by familiar stereotypes that resonate with the audience because they carry a kernel of truth. The well-known stories of folklore and myth are filled with archetypal characters that are universally familiar and embedded in our collective subconscious.

The word 'archetype' is Greek in origin and the psychologist Carl Gustav Jung was inspired by classical sources in his theory of the human psyche. Jung identified 12 archetypes that advertisers and marketing and brand consultants use today as building blocks in storytelling for their clients. We all intuitively understand archetypes and consequently they offer a shortcut to meaning for brands.

Can you identify an archetype that fits your favourite brand?

The 12 brand archetypes

1 **Magician:** The transformer
2 **Outlaw:** The rule breaker
3 **Jester:** The fun maker
4 **Lover:** The romantic
5 **Citizen / Regular person:** The friend
6 **Nurturer / Caregiver:** The homemaker
7 **Ruler:** The leader
8 **Creator:** The craftsman
9 **Innocent:** The optimist
10 **Sage:** The expert
11 **Champion / Hero:** The challenger
12 **Explorer:** The adventurer

Archetypes provide a benchmark of expectation to live up to and must be authentic or they will fail. They are a springboard to creating meaning in brands and they provide a broad brushstroke of colour.

It is important to remember that archetypes are not meant to be a blueprint for a strategy; they are intended as a method to tell the brand's unique story. Brands are not created by choosing an 'off-the-shelf' archetype and retrofitting the brand around the character, but their story can be given greater clarity by recognizing which character traits they most closely display.

The archetype model is a tool for communicating brand meaning, and your brand will ideally have many stories to tell. It is important to note that the archetype is not a fait accompli or a substitute for a brand strategy. It merely helps to frame your thinking and to provide a vehicle for communication. Your brand will exhibit different archetype qualities at different stages in its lifetime. For example, the celebrity chef Jamie Oliver is known as the 'Kitchen Crusader'. A 'crusader' is a hero archetype but he fits the nurturer archetype too, by wearing his heart on his sleeve and championing good food, healthy eating and nutrition. Jamie Oliver also embraces aspects of other archetypes, but above all he is the hero, fighting for the common good.

A good story begins with a strong premise, something that will capture the hearts and minds of its intended audience and has the potential to grow. Hollywood blockbuster films are only judged a real success when they are worthy of a sequel and spawn a franchise, like *Star Wars* and *Batman*, because big ideas make great stories that can run and run.

It is often stated that, in essence, there are really only seven basic plots: overcoming the monster; rags to riches; the quest; voyage and return; comedy; tragedy; and rebirth. Archetypal characters populate these stories and your brand's story may fit one of these scenarios on its journey to fulfilment. What story will your brand tell?

TIP *The greatest storytellers leave endings open, so make sure your brand is not an open-and-shut case.*

Summary

A brand is a collection of attributes measured by their mental, physical, emotional and soulful engagement. Our perception of brands is based on their past reputation, the experience they provide and our expectations for a mutually rewarding relationship.

Successful brands transcend their practical purpose to confer meaning and status to the consumer and gain significant market advantage when they are sincere, authentic and dependable. When consumers love a brand they build a deep emotional connection. This bond of loyalty is a strong advantage against market competitors.

As organizations and their portfolio of products and services expand, a clearly ordered system for managing brands is necessary. The branded house, house of brands and endorsed brand models help organizations to manage meaning and grow equity in their brands. Transparency and clarity are vital for all stakeholder groups including employees, suppliers and consumers.

SUNDAY

MONDAY

TUESDAY

WEDNESDAY

THURSDAY

FRIDAY

SATURDAY

Fact-check [Answers at the back]

1. Brands have existed for centuries. Which of these brands is the oldest?
   a) Levi Strauss ❑
   b) Cadbury ❑
   c) Birkenstock ❑
   d) Moët & Chandon ❑

2. What are employees at Disney resorts called?
   a) Magic Makers ❑
   b) Cast Members ❑
   c) Mickey's ❑
   d) Fun Makers ❑

3. What is ISO 10668?
   a) The world's first brand performance standard ❑
   b) The world's first brand valuation standard ❑
   c) The world's first brand identity standard ❑
   d) The world's first brand definition standard ❑

4. Who told *Marketing Week*, 'A brand is worth only what you are prepared to pay for it'?
   a) Walter Landor ❑
   b) Michael Peters ❑
   c) Wally Olins ❑
   d) William Bernbach ❑

5. Which of these categories is not considered by an ISO 10668 brand valuation?
   a) Legal analysis ❑
   b) Behavioural analysis ❑
   c) Financial analysis ❑
   d) Employee analysis ❑

6. What is a monolithic brand architecture model?
   a) A portfolio of individual brands each endorsed by a parent brand ❑
   b) A single brand consistently applied throughout a portfolio of businesses, products and services ❑
   c) A portfolio of individual brands owned by a low-profile parent brand ❑
   d) A portfolio of sub-brands that share a dependent family relationship to the parent brand ❑

7. Which brand architecture model fits the Nestlé Group?
   a) Single brand model ❑
   b) Endorsed brand model ❑
   c) Branded model ❑
   d) Sub-brand model ❑

8. Which team is responsible for the brand's success?
   a) Marketing department ❑
   b) Human resources department ❑
   c) Board of directors ❑
   d) All of these ❑

9. Which psychologist popularized the 12 archetypes?
   a) Carl Gustav Jung ❑
   b) Sigmund Freud ❑
   c) Ivan Pavlov ❑
   d) Jean Piaget ❑

10. How many plot lines are available to a brand storyteller?

a) Five ☐
b) Seven ☐
c) Ten ☐
d) 12 ☐

MONDAY

Define your brand strategy

The brand strategy is the brand's road map to success. It identifies *who* we are travelling with, *where* we are going, *why* it matters and *what* is required. There are lots of ways of getting from A to B and the brand strategy should pave a pathway with confidence and charisma. A bold brand strategy requires a combination of sound logic and a leap of inspired faith to take the brand where other brands have yet to venture.

Planning and research are key, as is the self-questioning courage to answer truthfully, 'Is this really possible?' The better prepared you are and the more you know about your destination, the greater your chances of success.

Today we will look at the key brand criteria for the brand strategy.

- Purpose – What does the brand do?
- Vision – What is the brand's ambition?
- Values – What does the brand stand for?
- Mission statement – How is the brand going to achieve its vision?
- Proposition – Why do I need the brand?
- Positioning – How does the brand compare with its competitors?
- Personality – What is the brand's character?
- Audience – Who is interested in the brand?

What are the key brand criteria?

A brand strategy is the plan for a brand's delivery and it answers the big questions: who, where, why, what and when? These essential questions are answered through the **key brand criteria**: purpose, vision, values, mission statement, proposition, positioning, personality and audience.

Purpose

How do you make the world a better place? What is your 'big idea'? What is the inspiration that drives you to succeed? What is the clear benefit your brand provides?

If you are left scratching your head at these questions, you have a problem, because successful brands have a well-defined sense of purpose. An authentic purpose is like a calling, or impulse; it is something you feel compelled to do and that you are passionate about. A clear sense of purpose is bigger than a charismatic leader and will outlast the management team. Political parties survive leadership changes because they are based on an immutable idea. A sense of purpose is attractive to customers, employees, investors and suppliers. Brands compete at the most primal level by the quality of their ideology. Successful brands provide an emotional value that exceeds their market price.

Who are you and what do you stand for? Is your purpose a compelling invitation to like-minded people? In an era when society has high expectations of corporate social responsibility (CSR), a purpose must engage all audiences, both from within the organization and from outside. Remember that your customers have a role to play in the future of the brand. Some of the most progressive, dynamic brands share their sense of purpose with their audience. For example, Innocent Drinks has an ambition to 'Make it easy for people to do themselves some good' and The Body Shop's ambition is to raise public consciousness of ethical issues and stop animal testing for cosmetics.

SUNDAY
MONDAY
TUESDAY
WEDNESDAY
THURSDAY
FRIDAY
SATURDAY

Considerations for identifying a shared purpose

- Is it an authentic sincere extension of who you are and your beliefs?
- A purpose is much bigger than just delivering a profit – it's more compelling if it makes the world a better place.
- A shared sense of purpose stimulates high levels of employee engagement and creates a strong sense of community.

> **TIP** *Ask yourself what your product or service does and why it should matter to anyone. A good cause can be infectious. What's yours?*

Vision

If purpose is the brand's 'big idea', then the brand vision is the 'big picture' of how that idea will blossom and thrive. As the saying goes, 'From small acorns, giant oaks grow.' The brand vision is an ambition for the future that should be both inspirational and achievable. It may be an aspiration for five or ten years' time and should have clear benefits for the organization and its extended community of customers and suppliers.

Considerations for setting the brand vision

- It must be succinct and easy to comprehend.
- Focus on the destination and not the journey.
- Avoid words like 'best', 'leading', 'first' and 'number one'.
- Management must champion and promote its message.
- It needs to be measurable with a clear moment of achievement.
- It cannot be too easy and must require a level of accomplishment.

> # Workshop exercise: Brand biography
>
> If you find it hard to come up with a vision for your brand, put yourself in the shoes of a writer who has been commissioned to write a biography of your brand in ten years' time. What would you expect to read about your brand? Who will be the heroes and villains, and what will be the life-changing events? Write a precis of the highs (and lows) of the brand and the journey it has taken over the imagined past ten years. This exercise should provide a stimulus for your brand vision.

A great vision can inspire and consolidate a community in a common goal. It is both emotional and passionate. Helping your audience to build a picture in their minds of what you are thinking makes it easier for them to imagine their place in fulfilling this ideal future.

Don't forget to celebrate when the brand vision is fulfilled, but don't rest on your laurels. Once you have completed the brand vision, it is important to set new achievement goals to motivate the brand to higher levels of success. Too many brands achieve their goals earlier than expected and then lose their sense of direction. It is essential to reappraise your long-term goals periodically for key stakeholder groups to remain engaged with the brand.

Visionary leadership

Martin Luther King's vision was so vivid that its ambition is seared into our collective consciousness. His vision towered above his goals of civil rights legislation and created an evocative picture of what success looked like with his now legendary 'I have a dream' speech wishing for racial harmony.

Values

A brand can be defined by its values and really stand for something.

Values are the compass that provides a direction through the moral maze of life. It is easier to make friends with people who share the same values and this is also true when it comes to choosing brands.

Values are the corporate conscience through which performance and culture can thrive in an organization. Values marshal how an organization behaves, they help focus on what matters most and they provide a strategy for dealing with a problem. In the event of a corporate crisis, it is typically the culture that is blamed and a new set of values is ushered in as a popular remedy. Values have become the panacea for all corporate woes. To be truly effective, these values must be relevant to all employee job descriptions and have the muscle to empower them. In short, corporate values guide employee behaviour.

Values can often become a list of clichés that are poorly defined and generic. Annual reports, corporate brochures and induction packs are bolstered with pages dedicated to corporate values. But how were these values arrived at originally and are they still relevant today?

The value of trust

Trust is an example of a commonly held value and it is one that should be implicit in every brand. But what exactly does 'trust' mean as a brand value and how is it defined inside and outside the organization? Can employees trust senior management to keep their word? Can the customer trust in the product or service?

In order to succeed and have relevance, values require the unreserved endorsement of the boardroom supported by clear evidence that the management team is practising what it preaches. These values will need to be interpreted and understood at an individual level so that employees can integrate them into their job descriptions.

If you are part of an established organization with a legacy of values, it could be time to re-evaluate their effectiveness. Choose a 'values focus group' from across the organization including representatives from senior management, the marketing and human resources teams and line managers. Ask the group if these existing values are capable of delivering a unique customer experience or only a generic one. If the legacy values are of the generic 'me too' variety, they will add nothing to the personality of the brand. Having too many values can be just as ineffective as having no values at all. It's no good if your employees have trouble recalling your values; it is better to keep them short and succinct and limited to a core number of five.

Considerations for choosing brand values

● Are the values sincere and memorable?
● Do these values help to differentiate the brand?
● Are the values relevant to the brand experience?

- Can employees realistically live up to these values?
- Do the values provoke measurable behaviours that will enhance or transform the brand's performance?

It may take several days to arrive at your new values system, but it will have a long-lasting and positive effect, so it is worth every effort to get it right. The publication of the new values will directly influence decisions for hiring employees, measuring their performance and awarding rewards.

Appoint 'values ambassadors' from all levels of the organization to disseminate the values across the workforce. Ensure that every employee is within reach of these values ambassadors, from senior management to temporary staff. Values are best shared and practised 'face to face' – you cannot expect them to thrive if they are buried away in a document.

Mission statement

The point of an effective mission statement is to summarize the key brand criteria in a brief but compelling declaration of ideally no more than 100 words. It is a strategic communication that should be clearly worded and understood by all. The mission statement clarifies what the brand does, its ambition for the future and what it stands for.

The key to writing the mission statement is to make it relevant. Think of old sailing ships, places of worship or civic buildings: they often have inscriptions and texts carved into their walls or displayed in prominent places. These remind the occupants that they are part of a community and to behave morally for the greater good. The complete mission statement or a part of it can be displayed in the reception, canteen, lifts, stairwell, common area or car park – in fact anywhere where it will catch people's eye and bring it to the front of their minds.

Considerations for writing a mission statement

- Research the mission statements of your favourite global brands and then ask yourself how well they match your experience of that brand.

- Summarize your key brand criteria and make it clear what function the brand fulfils.
- Leave movement for growth.
- Provide a measure for achievement.
- Keep it short and succinct.

Proposition

The brand proposition is the unique selling point (USP) or big point of difference that distinguishes the brand from its market competitors.

Considerations for developing a brand proposition

- Is it a barrier to market competitors?
- Is it a compelling reason why your customers need your brand?
- Is it succinct, short and to the point?
- Is it relevant, distinctive and truthful?

Workshop exercise: Brand proposition

The brand proposition is the big point of difference that makes the brand the obvious choice for its target consumer. This exercise is designed to get straight to the point that differentiates your brand.

In his best-selling book *Zag*, the writer and brand strategist Marty Neumeier calls this approach the 'onliness statement'. You should place your industry, product or service category in the first space in the statement and the unique point of difference that appeals to your customers in the second. Ask your working group to fill in the missing words.

Brand X is the only _____ that
_____.

The business landscape is constantly changing and it is advisable to check the brand proposition periodically for relevance to the presiding conditions.

Positioning

We all rank and categorize the ephemera, experiences and acquaintances of everyday life. Children have their best friends, teenagers rank their favourite chart music and adults recall their best holidays. Brand positioning primarily concerns the place a brand occupies in the customer's mind.

In a jostling marketplace, a competitive brand needs to be at the front of the queue in the consciousness of the consumer. Brand positioning is the deliberate effort to occupy the number one slot in its chosen category. This is often achieved merely by being the first and most visible brand in an emerging sector. As the sector grows and broadens, it becomes necessary to focus on a particular market segment and become the first choice for that audience.

A brand positioning map enables you to visualize the position of your business, products or services in relation to competing brands in your marketplace. The diagram illustrates a brand positioning map with the axes set to quality and price but you can change the axis measurement criteria according to your market requirements.

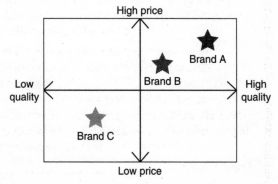

A brand positioning map

Brand mapping gives you the opportunity to see your brand in a marketplace context. Where is the opportunity for your brand to lead?

You may discover that you have identified a vacant brand position and decide to take the opportunity to become the first brand to occupy that space. Of course, the niche must be big enough to support your business but doing things differently can pay big dividends.

Personality

When considering the brand's personality, it is helpful to think of the brand as an archetype or famous person and imagine who they might be. Is there a prominent person of influence, a celebrity, a historical or fictional figure who best typifies your brand? The process of anthropomorphism – imagining your brand as a human – can help to give dimension to the brand.

Consistency and continuity are the hallmarks of well-managed brands. A deep understanding of how the brand will behave, in any given situation, is essential for any brand manager. The trick is to make sure that each and every touchpoint of the brand experience is delivered with consistent personality.

The brand's personality influences communication, behaviour and aesthetic style and the opportunity is to capitalize on it so that it becomes a valuable differentiator that offers a deeper relationship with the consumer. Products and services can easily be emulated, but a strong personality is much harder to copy. Some of the biggest global brands are extensions of their founder's personalities, for example Virgin's Sir Richard Branson.

The public face of the brand

The brand champion, brand mascot, brand ambassador, celebrity brand ambassador and brand advocate all influence the brand's personality. They must share an ethos and work together in the same spirit to deliver a consistent brand experience.

1 The brand champion: *the CEO or founder*

Positives: This is the person with whom the buck ultimately stops. They should be both inspiring and admirable and be highly knowledgeable about every aspect of the brand and where it is going in the future. Few of us are gifted natural speakers but a sincere passion for a subject will always be felt and it communicates as authentic.

Negatives: Not every CEO or founder is a natural people person and they may lack charisma. If they cannot connect with people emotionally, they may detract from the brand or, even worse, be a liability.

2 The brand mascot: *an anthropomorphic character*

Positives: Mascots can be witty and endearing and provide a face to an intangible commodity. They never grow old or behave out of character. They can become a valuable brand asset with merchandising possibilities, for example Michelin's Bibendum and Compare the Market's Aleksandr Meerkat.

Negatives: They are fictional and surreal and may detract from the truth. Their typically jovial nature may not be suitable for every brand.

3 The brand ambassador: *the engaged employee*

Positives: The employees of an organization are the best indicator of the brand's authenticity, or, in the words of the popular aphorism, 'We are only as good as our people.' Empowered employees can bring the brand to life and create strong touchpoint experiences for customers.

Negatives: If you do not recruit employees who share the same values and ethos as the brand, staff behaviour may detract from the reputation of the brand. Without the right induction or training, employees may feel disenfranchised from the notion of the brand and reflect this in their behaviour.

4 The celebrity brand ambassador: *the paid endorsement*

Positives: Celebrity endorsement of a brand can borrow equity and excitement from the celebrity. The celebrity can enhance the positioning of the product or service as a lifestyle brand.

Negatives: Celebrities can let you down. Details from their personal lives can creep into the news and contradict the values your brand stands for.

5 The brand advocate: *the loyal brand fan*

Positives: A referral from a friend or someone we trust can be the most effective introduction to a new brand. These vociferous consumers are an important aspect of the personality of the brand. They are the brand tribe leaders and they can attract like-minded people or repel detractors. Consumers can be the loudest voice of the brand, so embrace them and include them as the mouthpiece of the brand.

Negatives: Social media provide ample opportunities for consumers to voice their feelings about the brand, and these may not always be positive. Their comments and views can carry more weight than anything the brand would like to say.

Audience

The brand performs on a circular stage to a surrounding audience. The audience is drawn from many walks of life and their opinions of the brand contribute to its overall perception. Do you know who your customers really are, who you are working with and what organizations support you? The audience is never passive; it is an interactive community of people with an interest in the enterprise.

Workshop exercise: Audience

It is a helpful exercise to visualize a virtual audience radiating around the brand – based on its influences. Compile a list of all the various groups who interact with the brand. Depending on the type of organization, product or service, certain groups will have a greater impact on the brand than others.

Number each segment in order of importance in terms of impact on the success and long-term future of the brand. The illustration shows an example of a typical brand audience before any numbers have been assigned to the groups.

A typical brand audience could include the following interested parties: employees, management, resellers, advisers, competitors, charities, media, financiers, investors, government, associations, customers, prospects, suppliers and partners.

It is important to profile each audience sector before you take the brand to market. Consider the lifestyle habits of these 'influencers' and what's important and relevant to them. For example: what car do they drive, what newspaper do they read, what level of education do they have, and where do they live, shop, eat or holiday?

Next steps

Draft a preliminary brand strategy document addressing the key brand criteria in the light of the outcomes of your workshops. Circulate the document to your management team and key stakeholders for consideration.

It will be necessary to back the document up with clear communication throughout the organization. Employees must be informed immediately of any key changes to the organization that will affect the nature of their work and well-being. It is absolutely essential that the strategy is effectively communicated within the organization before any external parties have access to it, and it is common courtesy to inform employees of changes to their workplace before informing the news media.

The final document should then be shared across the team and disseminated through all line managers.

The next stage is to express this strategy through the brand's identity. The identity is the visible delivery system for the strategy, and we will go on to discuss this in Tuesday's chapter.

Summary

The key brand criteria are the essential elements of a brand strategy.

- Purpose – How do you make the world a better place? What need do you fulfil?
- Vision – A strong vision is a rallying cry to the audience to join the quest.
- Values – What do you stand for? What do you believe in?
- Mission statement – This statement consolidates the key brand criteria in a brief manifesto that is clear to its audience.
- Proposition – The unique selling point (USP) highlights the key point of difference that is hardest to emulate and provides the strongest barrier to competition.
- Positioning – In a crowded marketplace, positioning is about placing a brand at the forefront of consumer consideration.
- Personality – Strong brands have consistent personalities and a developed sense of self.
- Audience – Deep bonds of loyalty are earned when a brand understands its audience. If a brand tries to be 'all things to all men', it can spread its appeal too thinly.

Fact-check [Answers at the back]

1. On which original cause did The Body Shop build its brand?
   a) Support Community Fair Trade ❏
   b) Activate Self-esteem ❏
   c) Protect the Planet ❏
   d) Against Animal Testing ❏

2. Innocent Drinks has an ambition to 'make it easy for people...'
   a) ... to do themselves some good ❏
   b) ... to do the world some good ❏
   c) ... to do good ❏
   d) ... to do people some good ❏

3. What is the ideal maximum number of core values to have?
   a) Three ❏
   b) Five ❏
   c) Seven ❏
   d) Eight ❏

4. What should the mission statement summarize?
   a) Vision and values ❏
   b) Purpose and vision ❏
   c) Values and personality ❏
   d) Key brand criteria ❏

5. What is a USP?
   a) Unique sales position ❏
   b) United service proposition ❏
   c) Unique selling point ❏
   d) Uniting sales point ❏

6. What is the purpose of a brand positioning map?
   a) To identify the market position of competing brands ❏
   b) To identify the geographical position of brands ❏
   c) To identify the value of brands ❏
   d) To reveal brand loyalty ❏

7. Sir Richard Branson is the brand champion for which brand?
   a) British Airways ❏
   b) Vodafone ❏
   c) Sky ❏
   d) Virgin ❏

8. What is the brand mascot for Michelin called?
   a) Tony the Tiger ❏
   b) Bibendum ❏
   c) Wenlock ❏
   d) Zingy ❏

9. Who is Aleksandr Meerkat the brand mascot for?
   a) confused.com ❏
   b) gocompare.com ❏
   c) comparethemarket.com ❏
   d) moneysavingexpert.com ❏

10. Who forms a brand tribe?
   a) Employees ❏
   b) Celebrities ❏
   c) Management ❏
   d) Loyal brand fans ❏

TUESDAY

Express your brand through its identity

Since the start of civilization we have used names, signs and symbols to identify individuals and organizations. From national flags to crests on shields, what was once required for identification on a noisy battlefield is now needed for differentiation in a busy marketplace. Brand identity is the marketing equivalent of heraldry, and its elements – name, logo and colours – are powerful triggers that spark recognition of the brand in the marketplace.

Today we will consider the basic elements of a brand identity:

- Name – the brand's moniker, i.e. how it is known and referred to
- Strapline – the brand's motto; a quality statement of the brand
- Logo – the brand's signature mark, used to authenticate and identify
- Mascot – a symbolic characterization of the brand that may be drawn from nature
- Colour– the choice of colour or colours, forming the livery of the brand
- Typography – the brand's typeface; the handwriting of the brand
- Aesthetics – the brand's style, i.e. its look, feel and tone of voice.

Brand identity is essential for the differentiation, authentication and positioning of the brand. The outward expression of the identity projects a unique set of qualities to its audience that contribute to the overall perception of the brand.

What is brand identity?

The elements of a brand identity are designed and crafted to project an image of how the brand owner would like the product, service or organization to be perceived. The brand owner can control the design and form of these elements, but ultimately the consumer's opinion will be decided on the outcome of their experience. The basic elements of the brand identity (name, strapline, logo, mascot, colour, typography and aesthetics) only acquire value and significance through repeated and favourable association with the brand experience.

Name

Choosing the right name for a brand is like choosing a name for a baby: you want to give the brand the best start in life. Names come with preloaded meanings and associations that have the power to open some windows of opportunity and potentially close others. Getting the name right can give a brand an advantage.

If you build a good reputation associated with that name, it will become a valuable asset. The choice of colour, logo and visual imagery may evolve over time, but the brand name is the element least likely to change. However, should the brand fail or fall into disrepute, the existing brand name will become notorious and significantly devalued.

It takes a lot of effort and investment to implement and raise the awareness of a new name. In addition, name changes are often viewed with suspicion by financial institutions and investors and mocked by the media. If the old name ties the brand to an idea that is now unattractive or irrelevant, it could be time to change. Reasons for a name change include mergers and acquisitions, new ownership or management changes.

Considerations for choosing a brand name

● Does your choice of name support your key brand criteria? *Think about your purpose, vision, values, mission statement, proposition, positioning, personality and audience.*
● How will the name sound when spoken out loud and will it be easy to pronounce?
● Will it make sense in different languages and cultures?
● How will the name appear in black ink on a white page or illuminated on a mobile device?
● Is the name legally available? *Check Internet domain names, limited company names, trademarks and social media.*

Classification of names

Family names

Examples: John Lewis, WH Smith, Morgan Motor Company
Positives: Placing your family name on a product or service is one of the oldest forms of branding. The implication is that you are guaranteeing the efficacy of the product or service and personally endorsing it.
Negatives: If the brand fails, it will always be linked with your personal reputation. If you wish to sell the brand in the future, it may be less attractive because of the personal association.

Descriptive names

Examples: Toys 'R' Us, PC World, General Motors
Positives: A descriptive name makes it very clear which marketplace you are in.
Negatives: Descriptive names are generic and lack personality. The descriptive choice of name will pigeonhole the

brand and limit it to a particular niche, which may restrict the growth opportunities for the enterprise.

Invented names

Examples: Karrimor, Kangol, Kodak

Positives: An invented name can be memorable and easier to protect legally.

Negatives: It can take time to raise awareness of invented names and they may require a lot of marketing to achieve recognition.

Symbolic names

Examples: Jaguar, Shell, Puma

Positives: Names that borrow qualities from fictional or historic characters or that use flora or fauna as metaphors are able to capitalize on the associations those subjects already possess.

Negatives: Check that the metaphor is widely understood by your audience and does not have any unfortunate or less desirable meanings.

Abbreviated names

Examples: IBM, NASA, BA

Positives: The acronym is an effective way to shorten a long and difficult-to-remember name. Such names often arise following amalgamations of companies.

Negatives: A series of letters has little or no personality. Such names may prove difficult to protect legally.

Geographical names

Examples: Fuji, Jacobs Creek, Evian

Positives: It can be attractive to align a brand to a national or regional characteristic. Some nations and places are renowned for certain products. Examples include Swiss watches, German engineering and French wine.

Negatives: Any deterioration or a failure of international relations with the associated region could have negative consequences for the fate of the brand.

Foreign-sounding names

Examples: Berghaus, Häagen-Dazs, Gü

Positives: A made-up, foreign-sounding name may be used to leverage the value associated with the national or regional leadership for a particular product category.

Negatives: If your brand does not come from the region suggested by the name, you could be accused of trying to mislead the audience. In an era of corporate social responsibility (CSR) and a time when the sophisticated consumer wants to know the provenance of a product or service, this strategy could backfire.

Modular names

Examples: Apple iPhone, iMac, iPad

Positives: This strategy is often used when the core brand name has great equity and can be used as a prefix to other products and services. This can be a very effective strategy if your brand is branching out into different areas.

Negatives: Every time you apply your brand name to a new venture you risk weakening its overall power. If the new activity fails, it can have repercussions on the core business.

Strapline

A great strapline will summarize the brand's proposition, be memorable and be witty. Some of the most effective straplines have become part of popular culture and cultural idioms. The Ronseal wood stain campaign from 1994 – 'Does exactly what it says on the tin' – has become a popular phrase to describe anything that is uncomplicated and straightforward.

Writing a great strapline is an art form; it takes skill to summarize the proposition of the brand. The strapline clarifies the brand idea in a few words, typically no more than five. It is an opportunity to establish the brand's 'tone of voice' and will typically be the first words associated with the brand. The challenge for the writer is to communicate what the brand believes in, and its values and personality. It needs to be relevant to the consumer, authentic and straight to the point.

Considerations for writing an effective strapline

- Does the strapline support the key brand criteria? *Think again about your purpose, vision, values, mission statement, proposition, positioning, personality and audience.*
- Is it easy to remember? *Keep it short – around five words.*
- Is it emotional? *Make it positive but not belligerent.*
- Can it be legally protected? *It should be authentic, unique and credible.*

Logo

A logo is the signature of the brand; it identifies, authenticates and promises the brand experience wherever it is displayed. Logos are graphic devices that can be typographic, symbolic or abstract forms or a combination of all three.

The word 'logo' has become the default term for any graphic corporate identification device, but other specific terminology may also be used: avatar, colophon, emblem, icon, ideogram, logogram, logotype, monogram, pictograph, signature, trademark or wordmark.

A quick audit of the world's most valuable brands will reveal that there is no distinct format for a successful logo. Typographic wordmarks and symbolic ideograms sit side by side with brands that combine both symbols and words to equal effect. As a general rule, the one aesthetic they commonly share is simplicity because this helps them to be recognized in an instant. Highly valued global brands that use logos based on a combination of both symbol and type include Microsoft, HSBC and KFC.

Typographic logos

A typographic logo or wordmark is a unique relationship of alphabetical characters originated specifically for the brand. The characters are often custom-made but they may be inspired by an original typeface or handwriting. The brief for the designer is to create a distinctive letterform that represents the key brand criteria. Wordmarks are used by some of the world's biggest and most successful brands including Google, Coca-Cola and Disney.

Symbolic logos

Mankind has been creating symbols and imbuing them with meaning since the Palaeolithic era. Metaphorical symbols are an attractive source of inspiration for logos. Choosing a symbol from the Earth's flora, fauna or mineral wealth provides a seemingly infinite resource of imagery that is permeated with meaning. An oak tree can represent strength and a leaping cat suggests agility. Some of these symbols have left indelible marks in our collective consciousness. Aided by the nuance of design, the simplest abstract mark of a cross could have multiple meanings, for example faith, gallantry, first aid, peace, luck or fear. Some of the world's biggest brands, including Apple, Nike and Shell, are identified by a symbol.

Considerations for effective logo design

- **Appointing a designer**
  Choose a professional organization to help you with your brand identity and view their portfolio for evidence of originality. A clear brief will guide the creative solution towards a successful outcome, so agree the key brand criteria before proceeding to any creative work. Creativity thrives on oppression and a prescriptive brief can produce some of the most effective results.
- **Does the design satisfy the key brand criteria?**
  Relate it to your purpose, vision, values, mission statement, proposition, positioning, personality and audience.
- **Is the design too complicated?**
  The difference between good and bad design can be knowing when to stop. Multiple fonts, graduated colours and detailed images can be distracting. Some of the best logos are exercises in restraint and reflect the 'less is more' school of thought. Simplicity is key.
- **Is the design versatile enough to work across a variety of media?**
  Test the logo in black and white, view the design at extreme sizes online and offline, hand-draw it, engrave it – will it still be legible and identifiable?

- **How will the design look in print, online and on a mobile device?**
  The limitations of screen pixels can be unforgiving to details.
- **Will the design survive the test of time?**
  No one can predict the future but take care with fashion influences because they can date quickly.
- **Landscape or portrait?**
  Is the design available in both horizontal and vertical formats? How will the logo appear on a website, business card, promotional pen or pop-up exhibition stand? Consider the different applications of your brand and the most versatile format. Perhaps you may need to consider both landscape and portrait?
- **Have you trademarked it?**
  Your logo may grow into a widely recognized form that has real value, so it is prudent to protect yourself. To be trademarked, the design must be distinctive and not generic.

Mascot

Kellogg's Frosties' Tony the Tiger and Ronald McDonald, the McDonald's clown, are both examples of long-lived brand mascots. They succeed because they connect with their audience emotionally. A character mascot can bring a brand to life with humour and personality and give a face to the brand.

Brand mascots are particularly helpful when a product or service is intangible. A character mascot can animate the brand's attributes and values and can add a vibrant dimension to advertising, exhibitions and promotions. Energy companies and insurance groups have successfully created characters that help to position their brand in the heart of the consumer. Brand mascots can also appreciate into valuable assets with marketing and merchandising possibilities of their own, for example with their own fan club or Facebook page. Reproductions of mascots can become sought-after collectibles – early examples of Michelin's Bibendum are now collectible antiques.

Considerations for creating a brand mascot

- **Is the character relevant?**
  Does the mascot have a story to tell? Is the mascot based on the logo? How does it relate to the key brand criteria?
- **Have you trademarked the mascot?**
  To qualify, the mascot must be sufficiently distinctive, and the more abstract the relationship, the better. A good example is the Andrex puppy representing softness. Consider international filing for trademarks on exported brands – the Bibendum Michelin Man has trademark filings in over 100 countries.
- **How will it behave?**
  This is the embodiment of the brand and its voice, physical shape, energy and demeanour will all be judged as manifestations of the brand.

Colour

From the yellow and black stripes of a stinging insect to the seductive red of a strawberry, colour in nature communicates signals that are instantly understood. We can recognize colour faster than we read text and distinguish hues at greater distance than we can hear the spoken word. Colour is a valuable brand asset and some of the world's biggest brands have become inextricably linked to their choice of hue. Think of Coca-Cola's red, UPS's brown and IBM's nickname, 'Big Blue'. The opportunity for the brand is to 'own' the colour in the mind of the consumer. Coca-Cola's claim to red is so strong that they successfully rebranded Santa Claus in the early 1930s, creating the definitive image of Santa clad in brand-matching red robes.

The choice of colour may be symbolic, personal or psychologically influenced. Children will squabble over identical chocolate bars for their preferred colour wrapper. 'Showing your true colours' is a popular idiom that is used when describing someone who has revealed their true feelings. A carefully chosen colour palette is an immediate trigger for recognition.

So how do you choose a colour for success? There is an overwhelming preference for the colour blue in the world of business brands, but choosing a different colour that complements your key brand criteria can significantly help to differentiate your product or services.

Considerations for selecting a colour palette

- Does the target marketplace have a symbolic colour associated with it?
- Does the choice of colour reflect the brand positioning?
- Does the colour have an undesirable meaning in a different country?
- Does the colour reproduce consistently in print, on screen and in 3D applications?
- Will the colours convert to greyscale and remain clear?
- Will the choice of colour look dated in five years' time?
- Could the choice of colour palette be mistaken for another brand?

Typography

A graphologist can analyse an individual's handwriting to detect their character traits. A corporate typeface is the handwriting of the brand and we can all make assumptions about what an organization is like based on the typeface they use.

A carefully chosen typeface can project aspects of a brand's personality and enhance communication. Any branding programme must choose a typeface and bear in mind that it will be required to work in print, online and in 3D applications. The choice of typeface should be guided by the key brand criteria and match the brand's values and personality.

The majority of businesses restrict their typeface choice to the selection available on the operating system of their personal computers. Choosing a typeface from outside the narrow selection available on the latest version of Microsoft Windows® offers enormous scope for individuality. The drawback of purchasing a type style from outside the default Microsoft Windows® set is that user licences are required. Smaller businesses will be drawn to the economic merits of choosing a Microsoft Windows® typeface and the practicalities it affords for email, Microsoft PowerPoint and website compatibility. However, it is always worth considering a typeface choice from outside the standard set of operating system typefaces.

Consider choosing a typeface from outside the default selection on your personal computer. It can cost a bit more and involve licensing users, but it offers you far greater scope for individuality and originality.

Typeface categories

Since Johannes Gutenberg and the invention of moveable type in the 15th century, the choice of typeface designs and styles has grown exponentially. An officially recognized system of categorizing these typefaces has yet to be devised, but the simplest system to understand divides the broad groups of typeface styles into four categories: serif, sans serif, display and script.

Serif typefaces

Examples: Times, Garamond, Baskerville

The most identifiable characteristic of a serif typeface is the flared, ear-like endings of prominent letters. The general opinion is that serif typefaces help guide the eye when reading long lines of text.

Sans serif typefaces

Examples: Frutiger, Helvetica, Arial, Univers

'Sans' is a French word meaning 'without' and it describes a group of typefaces that do not feature serifs and are generally constant in the width of their stroke lines. Sans serif typeface designs are popular for signage systems and the Frutiger sans serif typeface designed by Adrian Frutiger is used in many of the world's airports.

Display typefaces

Examples: Arnold Böcklin, Rosewood, Critter

Certain display typefaces could equally be classified in the other categories mentioned here, but what unites them is their unsuitability for text use. Display typefaces are typically bold and decorative and are designed for use in headlines, titles and names. The examples named above are novelty and highly ornamental typefaces.

Script typefaces

Examples: Shelley, Mistral, Edwardian Script

Script or calligraphic typefaces are decorative and have the appearance of being handwritten by pen or brush. These typefaces are popular for invitations and events and are best used in specific situations with care and subtlety.

Considerations for choosing a typeface

● Think about the situations the typeface will be applied to: stationery, literature, online, signage, etc.

- Be careful that you choose a typeface with the right style for your brand. For example, Comic Sans is based on a handwritten style familiar to readers of comic books and it may be ideal for a nursery or a primary school but it could undermine the message for most businesses.
- Upper and lower case text is easier to read than all capital letters because the reader recognizes the shapes of the words.
- Regular upright roman type is easier to read than italic type.
- Use contrasting colours when using coloured type.
- Black text on a white background is easier to read than a pale colour 'reversed out' of a darker one (e.g. white on black).
- Exaggerated letter spacing and word spacing can compromise readability.
- Think about line length – wide widths of text are less readable than narrow columns.
- Restrict your choice of typefaces – too many styles can be chaotic.
- Serif typefaces are more legible for large quantities of text than sans serif.
- Using a text grid gives a publication a consistent feel that aids the reader.

Aesthetics

The aesthetics of the identity are its look, feel and tone of voice. Some of the world's biggest brands have a distinct look, feel and tone of voice that is immediately associated with the experience of the brand. Examples are Apple, Nike and Coca-Cola. These brands provide unique experiences that engage the senses and emotions. Their nuanced style of communication creates a strong 'aesthetic' linked with the brand experience.

Each working day, employees receive hundreds of emails commanding their attention. How they answer these messages and write new ones should be valued as frontline brand communication. But how often do we consider whether the messages and their tone of voice reflect the brand strategy?

Tribal aesthetics

The artist Grayson Perry created a series of six tapestries inspired by William Hogarth's series of paintings called *A Rake's Progress*. The work, called *The Vanity of Small Differences*, illustrates the brand aesthetics of each stratum of society in contemporary Britain. The working class, middle class and upper class are explored through their tastes, social habits and status symbols in a work that serves as a brand aesthetic mood board for British cultural tribes.

Can you think of a brand that you could recognize if it were stripped of its logo and packaging? Is a logo necessary and can a strong brand be identified by its behaviour and visual style alone? A Smeg fridge stands apart from its competitors with its bold use of colour, dimension and form. The Marlboro cigarette branding is so recognizable that it was able to sidestep the EU ruling outlawing tobacco advertising in sport: it used an abstract barcode device instead of its familiar logo on the Ferrari racing team's livery and was still able to be recognized before it was eventually removed.

A special language or vocabulary can be alienating or embarrassing to an outsider. 'Jargon' is specific words and phrases that obscure the meaning to people outside a particular group or profession, but using jargon is also a way of bonding customers to a brand. This is very effective in the area of youth culture, where building a cult audience can be a long-term marketing plan.

A brand's aesthetics are an essential part of its culture and we will investigate brand culture in Wednesday's chapter.

Summary

The basic elements of a brand's identity provide a toolkit for the recognition of the brand.

● Name – The choice of name should support the objectives of the key brand criteria.
● Strapline – A strapline, slogan or tagline has a valuable function as a descriptor and proposition statement.
● Logo – A logo is a unique graphic device for visual identification. It may combine type, symbol and abstract forms.
● Mascot – A brand mascot can add an emotional dimension to the brand.
● Colour – The specific use of a colour or combination of colours can be highly effective at distinguishing the brand.
● Typography – The considered use of a typeface lends order and personality to communications.
● Aesthetics – Strong brands provide unique experiences that can engage the senses and emotions.

SUNDAY
MONDAY
TUESDAY
WEDNESDAY
THURSDAY
FRIDAY
SATURDAY

Fact-check [Answers at the back]

1. What type of name is the brand name Kangol?
   a) Family ❏
   b) Descriptive ❏
   c) Invented ❏
   d) Symbolic ❏

2. 'Does exactly what it says on the tin' is the strapline for which brand?
   a) Heinz ❏
   b) Dulux ❏
   c) Ronseal ❏
   d) Crown Paints ❏

3. Which of these brands uses a wordmark?
   a) Apple ❏
   b) Google ❏
   c) Nike ❏
   d) Shell ❏

4. Which drinks brand effectively branded Santa Claus red?
   a) Pepsi Cola ❏
   b) Coca-Cola ❏
   c) Dr Pepper ❏
   d) Red Bull ❏

5. Which of these typefaces is sans serif?
   a) Garamond ❏
   b) Univers ❏
   c) Critter ❏
   d) Mistral ❏

6. Which typeface is commonly used for wayfinding at international airports?
   a) Frutiger ❏
   b) Edwardian Script ❏
   c) Comic Sans ❏
   d) Baskerville ❏

7. A colophon is a type of what?
   a) Sans serif typeface ❏
   b) Logo ❏
   c) Brand mascot ❏
   d) Display typeface ❏

8. Which typeface style is unsuitable for text use?
   a) Sans serif ❏
   b) Script ❏
   c) Serif ❏
   d) Display ❏

9. Which brand is known as 'Big Blue'?
   a) Twitter ❏
   b) IBM ❏
   c) Citibank ❏
   d) Dell ❏

10. Which tobacco brand found a creative solution to a change in advertising rules in sport?
   a) Marlboro ❏
   b) Rothmans ❏
   c) Benson & Hedges ❏
   d) Silk Cut ❏

WEDNESDAY

Evolve your brand culture

The parallels between the world's most successful brands and nations are clear; they have foundation stories, their own ethics, unique words, a sense of community, strong leaders, bold traditions and distinctive sensations. Branded organizations can manage their cultural assets to deliver deeper meaning to both employees and customers.

We will see today that the brand culture is made up of the following components:

- History – the origins of the brand
- Ethos – the ideology and values of the brand
- Language – how the brand communicates
- People – the community behind the brand
- Leadership – the brand's champions
- Traditions – unique behaviour connected with the brand
- Sensations – the senses
- Physical elements – buildings, environment and interiors.

If a brand really stands for something and conducts its affairs according to defined principles, it will stand a better chance of building a healthy culture and attracting sympathetic admirers who want to be a part of the brand's success.

What is brand culture?

Culture may be defined as the ideas, customs and social behaviour of a group of people. As a corporate brand grows and develops, its culture evolves, encompassing its history, ethos and behaviour. The brand culture has the potential to be an asset if it is valued, managed and curated with care.

By contrast, poor culture and the absence of values can lead to brand failure. This was was commonly blamed as the root cause of the spectacular fall from grace of some of the world's largest brands witnessed in the first decade of the new millennium. Household names and institutions fell into disrepute and some ceased to trade overnight.

History

The oral tradition is the age-old custom of sharing cultural history by word of mouth, from one generation to the next. This narrative approach to community history is still relevant today. If you can tell a compelling story of how your brand began and the motivations behind its origins, you will have a better chance of sharing the brand meaning with a wider audience. We are more likely to act on a personal recommendation than react to the words of a copywriter in an advertisement. If you've got a cracking story to tell, people will happily retell that story for free.

The careful curation of a brand's history can prove to be a tremendous resource. Stories are a great way of grabbing our attention and conveying ideas and important messages in a memorable format. We connect emotionally with history by empathizing with the people at the heart of historical events. A great story makes a deeper impression when we can personally identify with the people involved.

Considerations for writing your big story

- **Keep it simple**.
  Long rambling stories with no direction will not work.
- **Be credible.**
  Don't fabricate or fictionalize because the truth will always out.

- **Don't be afraid of your emotions.**
  The best stories pull the listener in when they can empathize with the plight of the protagonist.
- **Include an element of surprise.**
  Tell the listener something they did not know or would not expect to hear. These are the ingredients that make a story repeatable.
- **Make sense.**
  Stories are an effective way to demystify complex issues in a simple, easy-to-understand medium.

You could think about compiling a collection of stories, for example:

- the founder's story – *their personal motives and goals*
- the employees' story – *notable employees and their brand-affirming behaviour*
- the inside story – *fly-on-the-wall insights*
- the epiphany story – *the stories customers tell their friends that attract new followers.*

Ethos

Think of your favourite brand as a nation and ask yourself what its unifying ideology is. A brand's ethos, or belief system, will be derived from the strategy and based on its purpose, vision and values. Together these aspects of the brand strategy shape a set of principles that gives deeper meaning to the brand. Products and services may be easily mimicked but personality and ethics are difficult to fake. An ethical stance can define a brand and provide significant competitive advantage.

Corporate social responsibility (CSR) is the conscience of commerce and has become the 'must-have' policy for every large organization. A strong ethos can connect everyone in the organization to a common goal. In the Victorian era pioneering brands such as Rowntree and Cadbury exercised a moral obligation that they felt towards their employees by providing a better environment for them to work and live in. Many early industrialists – for example Andrew Carnegie, who built his wealth on iron – felt strongly about giving something back to society and financed the building of libraries, universities and museums. Acts of philanthropy benefit society but a media-savvy audience may view an organization's motives with cynicism if they are not relevant to the brand.

Brands that practise a strong ethos are more likely to develop an ongoing relationship with consumers who share the same concerns. Strongly held principles go hand in hand with integrity, and consumers are predisposed to trust a brand that maintains a consistent stance. For example, if you were operating in the fishing industry and wanted to build a brand based on 'fresh line-caught tuna', a campaigning stance focused on cleaner oceans would be relevant. Where brands are concerned, paying lip service is never acceptable and sincerity is always the key.

Considerations for developing your brand ethos

● **Raison d'être**
   This is 'the reason for being' that makes the brand the answer to someone else's need. Tap into that need and turn it into a cause.
● **Esprit de corps**
   An ethos can inspire and attract like-minded people who feel that the brand is sympathetic to an aspect of their own personality. This deep feeling of acknowledgement can lead to customer loyalty and, in some extreme cases, build an extended community or brand tribe.
● **Purpose, vision and values**
   These crucial elements of the brand strategy are the beating heart of the brands credo. They are the basis of its faith system and deliver the ethos.

Language

If a brand is based on personality, the words used in every communication are its voice and form its verbal identity. Brand language is the vocabulary and diction of the brand. Used carefully, it creates a deeper level of continuity in the expression and communication of the product or service. Word choice and vocal nuance can communicate an attitude that is as much a part of the brand's identity as its logo and name.

The name and strapline are the first steps in the verbal expression of the brand personality. The values and ethos will add passion to the voice and the brand positioning will provide its accent. Words are powerful and the language of brands can be infectious and creep into everyday use when it strikes a chord.

Words and personality

The words of the following straplines tell us something about the personality of these brands:

- **Apple:** Think Different
- **Avis:** We're number 2, we try harder
- **BMW:** The ultimate driving machine
- **Guinness:** Good things come to those who wait
- **Heinz:** Beanz Meanz Heinz
- **HSBC:** The world's local bank
- **John Lewis:** Never knowingly undersold
- **Marmite:** You either love it or hate it
- **Nike:** Just do it
- **Tesco:** Every little helps

It is important to develop a brand voice that is consistent with the projected image. If the voice keeps changing or switches tone from advertising to social media or brochures to the website, a split personality will emerge. It is advisable to develop brand language and copywriting guidelines to encourage consistent communication to avoid developing a brand with mixed messages.

Considerations for finding your brand voice

● **What kind of person is the brand?**
  If you find it difficult to imagine the brand as a person, ask yourself which member of The Beatles pop group it would be.
  - Ringo – cheeky, irreverent and happy-go-lucky
  - George – quiet, thoughtful and spiritual

61

- John – outspoken, bold and mercurial
- Paul – polite, optimistic and enthusiastic

● **What accent does the brand have?**

Do the vocabulary and tone of voice link the brand geographically to a region? The idiosyncratic use of words and their juxtaposition can place a brand in an era as well as a place. If the brand is linked to a renowned region or celebrates a long tradition, a local accent and dialogue could create an authentic voice and enhance the customer relationship.

● **What signature words does the brand use?**

Through repeated use of key words and phrases, a brand can build valuable mnemonic devices. For example, Disney is famous for the words 'Magic Kingdom' and 'Magical Moments' – these words bring the brand to life in the consumer's mind.

● **What age group is the brand?**

It can help to imagine what age group the brand is and how this relates to its audience.

- Teenager – chatty, cheeky, enthusiastic
- Young adult – proud, strong, independent
- Middle age – concerned, protective, sympathetic
- Senior – wise, mentor, methodical

People

Compelling brands create their own communities. Do you know who's in your brand tribe? Do they stay up late at night for the launch of your latest product? Would they queue in the pouring rain for you?

A strong brand culture can embrace a lifestyle choice. Brands like Apple are famous for their cult-like followers queuing outside their stores to be the first early adopters of their technology at the vanguard of geek chic. When brands acquire meaning, they become essential to the fabric of people's lives. The outdoor clothing brand Barbour is a tribal indicator for the middle classes in much the same way that Adidas is part of hip-hop culture. When a brand becomes wedded to lifestyle, it will attract deeper feelings of ownership and the opportunity for feedback and involvement increases.

People are fundamental to the success of any organization – they are its very embodiment – but do successful brands attract a certain type of employee as well as customer? Can a recruitment policy create a community of like-minded people? Employer branding is the practice of growing a brand so that it is equally attractive as a prospective employer as it is as a provider of products or services.

Considerations for your brand community

- **The fan club**
  This doesn't mean an actual fan club (although many brands do have fan clubs, including the Harley Owners Group (HOG) of Harley-Davidson). It is referring to the array of opportunities to engage and support the customer and audience, including Facebook, Twitter, Instagram, Tumblr, Pinterest and a whole host of social media. A proactive attitude to social media can encourage a meaningful dialogue with the brand community. Fans may start their own unofficial Facebook pages or Twitter accounts in honour of the brand.

- **The brand community**
  Who is interested? Providing a focus for enthusiastic admirers of the brand is a great way to exchange ideas about the development of the brand. Car and motorcycle brands have had their popular ownership clubs for many years. Now these communities are just as likely to be linked to food or insurance.

- **The big event**
  Create an event or sponsor one that provides an opportunity to bring the ethos of the brand to life, e.g. festivals, anniversaries, founder's days and national holidays.

Leadership

From the CEO and right through the organization via its line managers, strong brands thrive on bold, accountable leadership. Strong leadership is fundamental to the success of any brand. It is the role of the leader to champion the brand, conveying their passion and enthusiasm to employees, customers, suppliers and all stakeholder groups.

Traditions

Brands can create their own traditions and some leverage from the festive mood at seasonal occasions. For example, the Jif lemon juice brand has appropriated Shrove Tuesday with their advertising campaign 'Don't forget the pancakes on Jif lemon day'. Coca-Cola uses Santa at Christmas on packaging, advertising and their iconic Coca-Cola Christmas Truck events in December.

Considerations for starting a brand tradition

● Does it complement the brand vision?
● Is it true to the values of the brand?
● Does the event match the brand's personality?
● Is the event relevant to the brand?

Sensations

Think of your favourite brand, or the brand you hope to create, and ask yourself whether you could still identify this brand if you closed your eyes. Can a brand survive sensory deprivation?

Few brands use the power of sensory branding to full effect. Each sense provides the brand owner with a myriad of possibilities to create a unique experience.

TIP *If you think of your brand as a nation, could it be recognized by its sights and sounds? Could you identify your brand by the tastes and smells of its cuisine or the warmth of its people?*

Sight

It's unsurprising that sight is the sense that gets the most attention, from corporate identity to product design. Brands can be recognized at a distance or in a crowded environment by their use of colour and form. Packaging and the design of a product provide ample opportunity to develop iconic forms that are equally recognizable and have protectable intellectual property assets for the brand. Think of the London Tube map, the Fender Stratocaster guitar and the Coca-Cola bottle.

Question: Is the design of your product or service unique in form?

Sound

You may think that sound is irrelevant to your brand experience, but consider the soft sound of a car door closing or the default ringtone on your smartphone. These are examples of how sound contributes qualities that become a part of the subconscious brand experience.

Now consider the music an organization plays to waiting callers on their telephone line. Vivaldi's *The Four Seasons* has become the default sonic blueprint for 'call waiting', but is the choice of Vivaldi an indication of a brand that has missed an opportunity to deliver a better touchpoint?

Question: If you compare your brand to the top 40 selling songs, which song do you think matches your brand? It may stimulate a debate about the brand.

Touch

Our sense of touch plays a primary role in the evaluation and understanding of our environment. By touching an object, we discover its weight, dimensions, texture and temperature. These qualities inform our perception of the object and are equally true of a branded product. As the age-old saying goes, 'Feel the quality.'

Luxury brand owners are expert at seducing the customer through the sense of touch. Silk, velvet, leather and precious metals are all used to great effect to stimulate sensory satisfaction.

Question: You may not have a tangible product, but does the choice of paper your business stationery is printed on match the expectation of your brand?

Smell

A keynote scent might seem irrelevant for the intangible product or service brand, such as a mortgage or insurance company, but consider the staff, customers and suppliers who visit the organization's premises. Fresh coffee and flowers in reception, citrus scents in the rest rooms and a policy of not allowing people to eat at their desks can have a dramatic effect on personal comfort. Smell is a subtle tool that can have a huge effect on the perception of your brand culture.

Question: Is there a scent you can associate with your brand experience?

Taste

Outside the food and restaurant trade, taste may seem like the least likely sense to embrace, but consider how many cups of coffee and tea you have consumed in the course of a typical working week. If the quality of the coffee or tea is good, you feel welcome and valued. A bad cuppa suggests that the host or the employer does not care. Larger organizations may provide restaurant and catering facilities and the menu could have a bearing on the personality of the brand.

Question: Would you allow drink and snack beverage machines on your premises and, if so, what branded refreshments would they sell? Does this have a bearing on the personality of your brand?

Intuition

The sense of intuition has a huge influence on our choices in life; it's that gut feeling you get when something feels just right. We can sense when people are genuine and detect the difference between sincere and obsequious behaviour. If you consider your brand as a person and imbue it with human characteristics, you increase the opportunity for emotional engagement.

Authentic brands are genuine; they win our confidence and are understood instinctively, without conscious reasoning. How do you appeal to your customer's sense of intuition? Pay attention to the details and provide a consistent seamless experience that runs from initial brand promise through to every brand touchpoint like an invisible thread.

Question: Have you ever avoided a product or service because of a gut feeling, because your instinct guided you? What was wrong?

Physical elements

When archaeologists examine the physical evidence of ancient civilizations, they seek to reveal cultural insights from the remains of buildings, tools and artefacts. The materials and craft methods indicate the wealth and sophistication of the people concerned.

Today, some of the world's largest organizations are compared to nations in terms of power and influence. Their cultures are expressed through their people, products and buildings and the environment they occupy. It's not just the buildings, it's the interiors and the way they are furnished and function as a living and working space that tell us so much about how they treat their own people.

There is a growing trend for new businesses to create quirky working environments. Google is famous for its colourful bicycles helping employees get around its Mountain View campus in California, Red Bull has a giant slide at its London Soho office and Innocent Drinks has synthetic grass and garden furniture in its Fruit Towers headquarters.

Commerce is responsible for most of the beautiful buildings on our city skylines and brands are behind some of the more distinctive examples. The Midland Grand Hotel in London and the Chrysler Building in New York are brand statements from the early days of rail travel and the automobile. Brands continue to build and create statements of their power today. As organizations grow and evolve their own distinct culture, they will inevitably leave behind more evidence of their existence.

Think about the organizations that you have previously worked for. If they had reason to vacate their premises overnight, would there be any clues left that would tell a stranger what type of organization had been there? What cultural artefacts has your brand produced (including product and marketing) that are sufficiently unique that they could be identified as belonging to the brand?

Summary

The culture of an organization begins with its first employees and takes time to evolve. How it develops and grows will be determined by the strength of its ethics and values. A strong organizational culture can be one of the brand's most enviable assets, attracting both customers and the highest calibre of staff.

The brand's culture is composed of the following important elements:

- History – the story behind the brand, how it began and the key figures
- Ethos – the guiding principles that form an umbrella for its values
- Language – the voice and accent that reveal the brand's personality
- People – the people who bring the brand to life and embody its spirit
- Leadership – the leaders who inspire colleagues to build the brand
- Traditions – the special occasions that bring the brand community together
- Sensations – the distinctive sensory experiences associated with the brand
- Physical elements – the environment surrounding the brand.

SUNDAY
MONDAY
TUESDAY
WEDNESDAY
THURSDAY
FRIDAY
SATURDAY

Fact-check [Answers at the back]

1. Which of these chocolate brands is closely associated with the Victorian era of philanthropy?
   a) Lindt ❏
   b) Green & Black's ❏
   c) Rowntree ❏
   d) Hershey's ❏

2. Which motorcycle logo is one of the world's most popular tattoo designs?
   a) Honda ❏
   b) Kawasaki ❏
   c) Harley-Davidson ❏
   d) BMW ❏

3. 'You either love it or hate it' belongs to which popular brand?
   a) Bovril ❏
   b) Marmite ❏
   c) Vegemite ❏
   d) Nutella ❏

4. Which words are essential to Disney's brand vocabulary?
   a) A World of Adventure ❏
   b) Magical Moments ❏
   c) Action-packed ❏
   d) Laughter-filled ❏

5. The Adidas brand has close associations with which music scene?
   a) Hip hop ❏
   b) Heavy metal ❏
   c) Punk ❏
   d) New Romantics ❏

6. Which brand fan club is known as HOG?
   a) Honda Owners Group ❏
   b) Harley Owners Group ❏
   c) Husqvarna Owners Group ❏
   d) Hesketh Owners Group ❏

7. Which seasonal occasion is the Jif lemon juice brand associated with?
   a) Christmas Day ❏
   b) Thanksgiving ❏
   c) Shrove Tuesday ❏
   d) Halloween ❏

8. Which piece of classical music are you most likely to hear on 'call waiting'?
   a) Vivaldi's *The Four Seasons* ❏
   b) Holst's *The Planets* ❏
   c) Handel's *Water Music* ❏
   d) Tchaikovsky's *1812 Overture* ❏

9. What exciting feature does the Red Bull headquarters in London's Soho have?
   a) Swing ❏
   b) Skateboard park ❏
   c) Slide ❏
   d) Basketball court ❏

10. What is the name of Innocent Drinks' headquarters?
    a) Smoothie Towers ❏
    b) Fresh Towers ❏
    c) Healthy Towers ❏
    d) Fruit Towers ❏

THURSDAY

Build your employer brand

Today we will focus on building your employer brand. The employer brand is the fulfilment of the brand idea in a mutually beneficial relationship between employee and employer. A brand comes from within an organization; it is the heart and soul of a venture. The customer brand and the employer brand are the external and internal facets of the brand. If the brand does not thrive inside the organization, it cannot flourish outside.

The employer brand offers a unique employment experience that is designed to appeal to individuals who share the organization's values and are predisposed to flourish within its culture. A company with a strong employer brand will build a good reputation as a desirable place to work.

Employers and the human resources department have a vital role to play in building a brand by hiring people who will contribute to the brand's culture and live its values. Conscientious, engaged employees who exemplify the brand proposition deliver the best brand experiences. New staff cannot be expected to absorb this knowledge without an induction programme, training and the support of line managers.

What is employer branding?

The employer brand and the customer brand are different sides of the same coin. The two facets should support each other and their aims and strategy must be aligned in order to deliver a healthy and powerful brand. It would be counterproductive to create a separate brand strategy and identity for the employer brand because it is not a separate entity. The strong employer brand is an interpretation of the brand strategy that generates the behaviours necessary to deliver a great customer brand experience and attract, retain and engage the best employees.

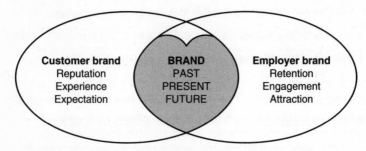

The healthy brand: a mutually aligned customer and employer brand

The key benefits of building a strong employer brand are to attract the best employees, engage them and retain them. Employer branding establishes a relationship built on trust by clearly communicating and practising the organization's deeply held beliefs. It inspires employees to deliver on the brand promise by behaving consistently according to its values and ethos.

Benefits of employer branding

- Low recruitment costs
- High employee retention
- Engaged employees
- Increased profitability
- Happy customers

The brand that you work for is the brand that you are most likely to discuss with your family and friends. Employees, alumni and job candidates have a significant influence on the wider perception of an organization as an attractive place to work. They are honest indicators of the corporate culture behind the brand.

Consider the questions we typically ask our friends and family about their employer. These questions have the combined effect of testing the brand's integrity:

- Are they a good employer?
- What's the pay like?
- How many days' holiday do you get?
- How do they reward their staff?
- Do they have a great pension plan?
- Are the promotion prospects good?

The brand and human resources

Marketing and human resources (HR) departments are most effective when they work together to deliver an integrated model of internal and external brand management. Human resources have a fundamental role in ensuring that the brand's values are clear and robust enough to drive the employee behaviours needed to deliver the brand. For example, the Disney brand has a clear set of values that provide employees or 'cast members' with a moral compass to deliver the brand promise of 'Magical Moments'. Each Disney employee is empowered to create unscripted moments of magic for the visitors to their resorts.

The HR role in building a strong employer brand

- Attract employees who share the brand's values.
- Retain employees who are a good cultural fit.
- Engage employees with inspirational and relevant training.
- Provide an employee experience as unique as the customers' experience.
- Reward and recognize employees who are good brand ambassadors.

Brand champion

The 'brand champion' is the public face of the brand and it's their duty to set a good example. This role is usually filled by the Chief Executive Officer, Managing Director or business owner and, if they cannot get passionate and enthusiastic about their own business, who will?

As the brand champion, their duty is to inspire the workforce and motivate them to do their best. They should ideally have the ability to energize people and evangelize the brand message so that it is clearly heard. The brand will be powerless if its ethos never leaves the boardroom – it needs to be shared and made accessible throughout the organization. The brand champion should acknowledge and encourage their employees, excite their customers and lead with conviction and vision.

Line managers

Line managers have a professional responsibility to uphold the best possible example of brand behaviour. They must take care that their emotional state does not adversely affect the brand experience. It is their duty to prevent their extreme feelings from affecting their colleagues and customers; this includes negative prejudices as well as preferential treatment.

Line managers have a special role to play in bringing the brand to life. They need to ensure that everyone they are responsible for understands and 'lives the brand', so that it permeates through every level of the organization. Line managers facilitate the dissemination of brand information and create natural brand ambassadors through their influence and example.

Brand ambassadors

'Brand ambassadors' provide a personal connection to the brand. The term is often used in connection with paid celebrities who are appointed for their distinctive qualities to advertise the brand. However, the least heralded but most important advocates are the employees who work for the brand on a daily basis. These brand ambassadors are the employees who bring the brand strategy to life for their customers, suppliers and shareholders and provide a personal connection.

Brands with strong values appeal to both employees and customers, but what happens when the brand's values are put to the test by operational efficiency? For example, in the logistics and express industry for fast delivery services, the customer experience can be a differentiator. If personnel are set unrealistic delivery targets for each day, the customer experience may be severely compromised by a rushed service. This puts extreme pressure on the employee to decide which is more important – a fast delivery or a good customer experience. The difference between what a brand says it is and what it actually does may lead to disappointment for employee and customer alike. If you consider the bad customer experiences that you have had in the past, it would not be surprising if poor customer service were behind most of them.

TIP *The adage 'The customer is king' is a reminder to complacent brands that customers can always take their patronage somewhere else.*

The employees of any brand are a measure of its values and their behaviour will be a test of its integrity. It makes good business sense to ensure that each member of staff is aware of the brand strategy, its history, what it stands for and their role in delivering the brand proposition. Employees can only advocate the brand when they fully understand it and line managers can play a crucial role in its dissemination.

Valuing alumni

The value of previous employees or 'alumni' is often overlooked and yet they offer great potential to become long-term ambassadors for a brand as their career progresses working for other organizations. Alumni have every right to be proud of their previous employer and should expect that the brand will add value to their CV when they apply to future employers. Retired employees are a valuable potential resource as mentors and an alumni network can provide an opportunity to mix with people who implicitly understand the brand and add weight to its culture.

The language an organization uses to describe its workforce can reveal a lot about the brand's culture. Google shares the spirit of 'Googliness' with its staff, who are known as 'Googlers' or 'Newglers' if they are interns. Nike has a team of brand experts called 'Ekins', the restaurant chain Nando's calls its team members 'Nandocas' and the London 2012 Olympic Games had 'Games Makers'.

Managers cannot realistically oversee every detail and they must therefore trust and empower their colleagues so that they instinctively know what is 'on' or 'off' brand. Happy and knowledgeable employees can become the reason customers keep returning and even one instance of exceptional service can leave a deep and positive impression in the customer's memory.

Brand engagement at the Olympics

The Games Makers at the London 2012 Olympic Games were a masterclass in brand engagement. In a relatively short time a strong team of volunteers was mobilized who went on to be credited with making the Games the outstanding success they were.

The International Olympic Committee President Jacques Rogge paid a special compliment to the Games Makers in his closing speech at the end of the Games: 'We will never forget the smiles, the kindness and the support of the wonderful volunteers, the much-needed heroes of these Games.' They were empowered and given freedom to act upon instinct in their personal interpretation of the Olympic brand.

Recruitment

The strong employer brand provides an organizational culture clearly defined by its values. These brand values provide a moral compass for employees, empowering them to act with confidence to deliver the brand experience. To create a strong corporate culture, it makes sense to recruit employees who already share the brand's values and are instinctively able to 'live the brand'. Lifestyle, leisure pursuits, charitable commitments, hobbies and interests will all provide evidence of a candidate's personal values and can offer a clearer indication of employment suitability than academic results alone.

The candidate experience during the job application process is a critical stage in the applicant's confirmation of the brand. If brands expect to attract the best talent, they must consider how they treat all applicants for vacant positions, whether they are suitably matched or not. Every applicant will expect to be given respectful treatment in accordance with the values of the brand. A poor experience may leave applicants with bad feelings that could be shared with their friends and family.

Employee engagement begins at the job application stage. We have come a long way from on-site noticeboards and newspaper job advertisements. Digital media allow a powerful targeted approach to recruitment advertising through social media, including Facebook, Twitter, LinkedIn and YouTube.

With the widespread success of these online services, there is a risk that the automated recruitment process can reduce applicants to commodities. The lack of personal contact and basic manners may leave many hopeful applicants with a negative experience.

Employer brand proposition (EBP)

What is the biggest reason why a potential employee should consider your organization as a place to work? The employer brand proposition (EBP) is the main point of difference between your employer brand and other businesses competing for the same candidates in the jobs market. The EBP should be aligned with the brand proposition defined in the brand strategy because the employees make the brand proposition viable.

Workshop exercise: EBP

Identify the single factor that is hardest to copy in your industry sector and adds value to your employer brand. What is it that you can offer a prospective employee that no other employer brand can? It should provide equal benefit to the employer brand and the customer brand and be authentic. This is the big reason that makes the employer brand such an attractive proposition and must appeal to all employees.

You can use the unique selling point (USP) exercise from Monday's strategy chapter to craft an employer brand proposition. Place your industry sector in the first space and your point of difference that appeals to employees in the second.

Employer brand X is the only _____
_____ that _____.

Employee value proposition (EVP)

The employee value proposition (EVP) tailors the EBP to the individual employee's job description. Every employee will have a different perspective of the brand according to their unique situation, including gender, age, culture and qualifications.

The EVP is a contract between the employer and the employee that clearly explains what is expected from each party. It articulates what the employer is offering in exchange for the employee's productivity, engagement and ongoing commitment. The ideal is to create customized EVPs for different sectors and pay scales. The EVP covers every aspect of the employment experience: ethos, values and culture plus the total rewards programme (compensation, benefits, work-life balance, performance and recognition, development and career opportunities).

Induction

An induction programme is the process of familiarization and settling into an organization and it is focused on the employee experience. The sustainability of a strong employer brand requires careful consideration of the employee experience from their first day and throughout their employment life cycle.

Without an induction, new employees get off to a poor start and may never fully understand their role in the organization. This can lead to poor team integration, low morale and ultimately a drop in productivity. Their experience will be a poor indication of the employer brand and will affect the organization's reputation.

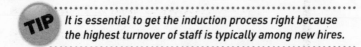
An effective induction starts on day one of a new job, typically lasts a couple of days and should make new employees feel welcome and valued. Most induction programmes explain brand values and culture. Computer gaming techniques are becoming popular with larger organizations to give employees experience of different touchpoint scenarios. This helps new employees understand what constitutes on-brand or off-brand behaviour.

Induction at Dyson

New employees at the consumer electronic brand Dyson are expected to assemble a vacuum cleaner from its component parts as part of their induction process. James Dyson told the *Harvard Business Review*, 'It gives them confidence in the technology. They know what's inside. And they keep the ones they build. It's to emphasize that what we do is make products that people use.' This approach to induction creates a special brand experience that won't be forgotten.

Learning and development

Learning and development (L&D) is essential for the engagement of employees, the effectiveness of teams and the performance of the organization. Placing an emphasis on education will empower the organization to achieve improved results. If employees are an organization's greatest asset, it makes sense to invest in them and develop their talents.

L&D is at the heart of engagement and fosters an energized, loyal and performance-orientated culture. All employees must receive adequate training in the use of the tools of their trade. Gaining new skills and qualifications can provide an employee with greater choices and career aspirations.

SUNDAY

MONDAY

TUESDAY

WEDNESDAY

THURSDAY

FRIDAY

SATURDAY

The employer brand benefits of an L&D programme

- Skilled employees produce better products and services.
- Employee engagement is boosted.
- Employees improve their career prospects.
- Organizational performance is increased.
- It leads to satisfied customers.

Employee engagement

Employee engagement is the balance between emotional attachment to the organization and individual job satisfaction.

There is a frequently told story that John F. Kennedy allegedly made an unannounced visit to the Cape Canaveral Space Centre during the Apollo Space Program. He approached three men in overalls and asked each in turn what they were doing. The first replied that he was 'earning a living', the second replied that he 'cleaned away all the rubbish' and the third replied with a smile that he was 'helping to put a man on the moon'. The third man displays all the attributes of an engaged employee, someone who feels a direct link between the job they do and the achievement of the organization.

Satisfaction (I love my job) + Contribution (I help my business achieve its goals) = Engagement

SATISFACTION
I love my job

+

CONTRIBUTION
I help my business
achieve its goals

=

ENGAGEMENT

Employee engagement

The reasons for a lack of engagement include poor leadership, weak communication and a lack of understanding about the brand. The combination of long working hours, frozen pay scales, lunch breaks at desks and the intrusive access of digital communication can create a resentful workforce. Health, prospects and a sincere interest in the welfare of the employee are critical. People are engaged when they like their work, they understand its value and they enjoy working with their colleagues.

Effective employee engagement enables employees to realize their full potential at work. To enable this they must feel respected, included, listened to and valued by their colleagues and line managers. Engaged employees find a sense of belonging in their organization and are inspired to put their best efforts into making it a success. High levels of employee engagement are linked with increased operational efficiency and reduced loss from theft and errors.

The benefits of employee engagement

- A shared feeling of pride and inclusiveness
- Employee contentment with career and future prospects
- Proactive positive and helpful attitude
- Improved health and well-being
- Lower absence rates
- Employees living the brand values

Reward and recognition

Studies reveal that 'Generation Y' or 'Millennials' are more likely to discuss with their friends and colleagues what they are getting paid, so transparent fairness is important to avoid resentment. It has become increasingly easy to determine whether you are being fairly remunerated and the online resource PayScale.com makes salary information available for comparison.

The saying 'Find a job that you love and you will never have to work again' may have some truth in it for those of us who are fortunate enough to find a true vocation. Whether you love your job or not, recognition plays an important part in performance.

TIP *A few well-chosen words of praise and encouragement at the right moment from a line manager will go further to boost morale than an 'Employee of the month' award.*

Values should ideally be used in the employee review process as a measure of performance for the purpose of reward and recognition. Celebrated employees are an opportunity to highlight the effectiveness of the employer brand and raise the profile of the organization. Rewards programmes can build brands by inspiring employees to realize the organization's mission and reinforce its strategic objectives. Most employees want to find meaning and purpose in their careers. It's important that any reward or act of recognition supports the values and ethos of the brand.

Summary

It is no coincidence that some of the world's most successful brands are also the most desirable organizations to work for. Certain brand names will always look good on your CV. A strong employer brand is beneficial in attracting and retaining the best candidates. The cost of replacing staff is a considerable expenditure for most organizations and, if a company can maintain a lower staff turnover than its market competitors, it will see a resulting increase in company profitability.

Informed, sincere employees add an emotional dimension that no sales brochure or website can ever provide. A business can create an experience that is harder to emulate by attracting and retaining engaged people who exemplify the brand's values. Employees really do have the potential to be a brand's greatest asset.

SUNDAY
MONDAY
TUESDAY
WEDNESDAY
THURSDAY
FRIDAY
SATURDAY

Fact-check [Answers at the back]

1. What is an employer brand?
a) A recruitment agency brand ❏
b) A separate brand for employees ❏
c) An HR brand ❏
d) A mutually beneficial relationship between employer and employee that fulfils the brand idea ❏

2. What is the primary role of HR in employer branding?
a) To fire bad employees who are a poor cultural fit ❏
b) To conduct annual performance reviews ❏
c) To attract, retain and engage staff who are a good cultural fit ❏
d) To manage L&D programmes ❏

3. What are the benefits of employer branding?
a) Lower recruitment costs ❏
b) Higher employee retention ❏
c) Engaged employees ❏
d) All of the above ❏

4. Who is the 'brand champion'?
a) A paid celebrity who endorses the brand ❏
b) A happy customer ❏
c) The CEO or business owner ❏
d) Employee of the month ❏

5. What are Nike's brand ambassadors called?
a) Ekins ❏
b) Nikesters ❏
c) Crepes ❏
d) Swooshes ❏

6. What is employee engagement?
a) Staff who love their job and value their contribution to the organization's success ❏
b) A contract of temporary employment ❏
c) A business relationship ❏
d) A business event for employees ❏

7. What is an EBP?
a) Engagement brand proposition ❏
b) Employee brand proposition ❏
c) Employer brand proposition ❏
d) Engagement brand policy ❏

8. What is an EVP?
a) Engaged vision proposition ❏
b) Employee value proposition ❏
c) Employer value proposition ❏
d) Engaged values proposition ❏

9. What is Glassdoor?
a) The invisible barrier preventing staff mobility ❏
b) The segregation of employees by hierarchy ❏
c) A social media service providing an inside look at businesses ❏
d) An intern programme ❏

10. Who are Generation Y?
a) People born between 1980 and 2000 ❏
b) People born between 1960 and 1980 ❏
c) People born between 1940 and 1960 ❏
d) People born between 1990 and 2010 ❏

SUNDAY · MONDAY · TUESDAY · WEDNESDAY · THURSDAY · FRIDAY · SATURDAY

FRIDAY

The importance of design

When design is at the heart of an organization, it is fundamental to the brand experience and not just a veneer or afterthought. Organizations that believe in design place designers at board level, for example Sir Jonathan Ive at Apple and Christopher Bailey at Burberry. Sadly, too many businesses treat design as a final gloss solution instead of a primary concern. Too often, design is treated as something you do at the end of a job for a quick-fix tidy-up. Design is not an add-on service; it is central to the business, and its success depends on its involvement from the beginning. Design provides the competitive advantage that distinguishes a business, product or service from its marketplace competitors.

Consumers are willing to pay a premium for products and services that are emotionally important to them. Design is often the most important differentiator when competing on price, performance and benefits because design creates the clearest points of difference.

Why is design important?

Design has an impact on every moment of every day, from the shape of a toothbrush to the design of a cereal packet, the train that we commute to work on and the desk that we work at. Designers affect our lives and some make our world easier to navigate: for example, we use Harry Beck's London Tube map and Jock Kinneir and Margaret Calvert's information design system for UK road signs.

Everything made by humans is affected by design. Design can transform business processes, systems and the organizational structure as well as branded products and services. The greater the value that is placed upon design, the more value it will return to the brand. Design can be used in every experience and should be looked at from the point of view of the customer, the employee and the supplier.

Luxury brands target consumers with a higher disposable income but also appeal to people who are 'in the know' or wish to be seen as part of a tribe. Buying the right brand of denim jeans or driving the right brand of car, for instance, can play on the insecurities of society or confer status and meaning. Good design can add considerable value to a product. Just think of the market for luxury handbags: consumers are prepared to pay high premiums for luxury handbags because the brands have social significance. These purchases have what is called 'sign value', as identified by the object value system.

The object value system

The object value system was devised by the French philosopher Jean Baudrillard for evaluating the consumer society. Baudrillard felt that consumption rather than production was the main thrust of capitalism. He argued that consumer desires were constructed rather than innate and that every purchase decision has a social significance behind it. The choice of brand will say something meaningful about the consumer.

According to Baudrillard's system, the value of a brand may be practical, economic, sentimental or social, and he identified four value-making processes.

Baudrillard's four value-making processes

1 **Functional value** – the practical purpose, e.g. a watch tells the time and a car is used for transport
2 **Exchange value** – the economic value, e.g. a watch may be worth a week's work and a car is equal to a year's salary
3 **Symbolic value** – the sentimental value, e.g. a watch may commemorate a retirement and a first car may celebrate passing the driving test
4 **Sign value** – position relative to a system of quality, e.g. an expensive Swiss chronograph watch may signify elitism and a prestige car may be an indicator of wealth

What is good design?

At the height of his success in the 1970s, the German industrial designer Dieter Rams asked himself this question: 'Is my design good design?' Concerned that he was adding to the problems of the world, he addressed his conscience and wrote the 'Ten principles for good design'. The principles tackle important concerns for every designer: innovation, usability, aesthetics, coherence, restraint, honesty, durability, accuracy, environmental impact and simplicity. These guidelines have affectionately been referred to as the 'ten commandments of design' and they continue to provide a reference for conscientious designers.

The clean lines of Dieter Rams' designs and their functional simplicity helped turn the German consumer electronics brand Braun into an international household name. His 'less but better' aesthetic has since been recognized as an important influence on the work of Sir Jonathan Ive, the Senior Vice President of Design at Apple.

Design and art

Because design shares a similar cultural status to that of art, its leading practitioners are often venerated like eminent artists. Notable examples are the 19th-century designer William Morris, a prominent exponent of the Arts and Crafts Movement and, in the 20th century, Raymond Loewy, the father of industrial design. Thomas Heatherwick's theatrical London 2012 Olympic Cauldron, Philippe Starck's sculptural orange juicer and Sir Jonathan Ive's industry-changing iMac personal computer have all pushed design beyond mere function to create celebrated works of art.

Design value

Sceptics who doubt the value of design should consider the transformation of the Samsung brand and the fortunes of South Korea. The booming economic growth of South Korea in relation to its geographical size and population may be attributed to its commitment to design and innovation.

In 1993 Samsung's Chairman Kun-Hee Lee travelled through Asia, the United States and Europe observing how consumers viewed his products. He was disappointed by the results and called his managers to a Frankfurt hotel to hear his vision of the future. The occasion became known as the 'Frankfurt Declaration' and his address was transcribed and distributed to employees with the famous rallying call, 'Change everything except your spouse and family.'

This programme of renewal included a new design school in the capital, Seoul, the Innovative Design Lab of Samsung (IDS). Samsung's brand revolution paid off and, within a decade, the brand was winning international design awards and it has since been celebrated as one of the most valuable global brands. The growth of Samsung and the bold changes it made in the early 1990s transformed the organization from the value sector to a respected and desirable brand in its own right.

Operational benefits of design

- Market-differentiated products and services
- Improved quality of products and services
- Enhanced corporate reputation
- Reduced manufacturing costs
- Increased market share
- Exporting opportunities
- Higher profit margins
- Increased brand value

Brand design

Design is integral to the success of every enterprise and its many disciplines include graphics, packaging, product, furniture, interior, interactive, web, vehicle, retail, building, fashion and textiles. Graphic design is the area of design that most marketing professionals are likely to have experience of. If you are in the process of creating a new brand or rebranding an existing organization, product or service, graphic design will be an essential consideration. From business cards to letterheads, packaging to websites, graphic design affects the fundamental necessities of any business.

'A logo is not a brand' has become something of a mantra, but don't let that undermine its value. The logo and its associated elements of the brand identity will get a lot of attention during the lifetime of the brand. Its careful design and execution will be an indicator to the audience of the type of experience they are likely to receive. The logo is a valuable brand asset that accrues meaning through its association with the brand experience. It's the big arrow pointing at the brand and assuring the audience that the product or service is authentic. Design agencies and brand consultancies invest a lot of time working on these elements to get them right. The basic elements of the brand identity include: name, strapline, logo, colour and typography.

Choosing a design partner

The design of a brand identity requires specialist design experience and creative skills. It would be unusual for an organization to have all of these skills available in-house. Choosing the right creative team is similar to choosing any professional service. First review their portfolio, research their reputation, evaluate their fees and then judge whether the personal chemistry is good for a working relationship.

The creative brand team's brief is to deliver a brand identity that communicates the key brand criteria of the brand strategy: purpose, vision, values, mission statement, proposition, positioning, personality and audience. Many brand consultancies and design groups will also offer a strategy service. It is essential that the creative team is briefed on the approved brand strategy because these are the agreed principles of the brand. An attractive identity with no relevance will prove insubstantial and meaningless.

It is fundamental that the brand strategy has been established before any creative conceptualization begins.

Creative thinking

It is typical for a design team to run a workshop with the client's management team to help find inspiration for the visual realization of the brand strategy. The creative team may use some creative thinking exercises to stimulate the creative process. The following exercises may be useful.

Creative exercise 1: Postcards

Place a selection of picture postcards in a pile in the centre of a table and ask the management team to choose one that expresses their idea of their organization as it is now and choose a second one to describe how they would ideally like it to be.

This never fails to get some very interesting results. People who are unused to thinking laterally are forced to think in an abstract way. The answers reveal much about the individual and their situation. The exercise demonstrates how we all see things differently: some people will choose an image for its literal meaning and others will choose an image for a metaphorical meaning.

Creative exercise 2: Brands

Ask your team to talk individually about their favourite brands and describe what they mean to them. This is balanced with the brand that they most dislike and a reason behind their answer. These questions should be answered instinctively and without deliberation.

It is important to understand the reasons for the client's choices. For example, are the answers based on details like the typeface, symbol and colour or are they more to do with the people behind the brand(s) and what they stand for?

Creative exercise 3: Symbolism

Explore the management team's feelings towards colour and symbolism. Ask your team to think in an abstract way about what could represent their brand, be it flora, fauna or colour. When you consider nations and sporting teams their identity is often very symbolic – the blues, the reds, a lion or a rose.

Creative exercise 4: On-brand/off-brand

'On-brand/off-brand' is like a parlour game and it forces the management team to consider how their brand would manifest itself in a series of abstract scenarios. The aim is to pinpoint what would be 'on-brand' and what would be the opposite or 'off-brand'.

This exercise explores the type of imagery that would be suitable to use for an advertising campaign or marketing promotion to support the brand. It is effective at getting into the psychology of the brand and what it stands for.

The scenarios suggested here may at first seem a bit strange, but they can be an effective way to get a debate going about what exactly represents the brand and best communicates the brand's strategy. If you prefer, you can try some scenarios of your own.

What type is your brand?

The following scenarios are suggestions for group consideration.

What would your brand be if asked the following questions?

- What type of sport? e.g. rugby, tennis, cricket, etc.
- What type of dog? e.g. Labrador, German shepherd, poodle, etc.
- What type of tree? e.g. oak, bonsai, willow, etc.
- What type of music? e.g. rock, classical, jazz, etc.
- What type of food? e.g. salmon, sushi, cod and chips, etc.

Creative exercise 5: Mood board

This hands-on exercise requires the management team to collect images or objects that they feel represent their idea of the brand. They can cut out magazine or newspaper articles or provide their own photographs. It can help to ask them to bring an object that appeals to their notion of the brand and tell a story to support the brand strategy.

The images, objects and stories will then be discussed by the group and judged on their merits. The approved material will be collated and may influence the brand's direction.

Creative exercise 6: Pinterest

It can prove useful to set aside a space or room where all the initial idea generation and collected ephemera can be placed for contemplation. If this is not possible, the social media content-sharing service Pinterest allows users to upload their own photographs or 'pin' digital references from websites and video-sharing services to a virtual pinboard.

This is a great design boon and groups can create a private board where all the accumulated assets and links to suitable material can be maintained. It is easy to share and allows the group to vote for or against items until the references are whittled down to the very essence of the brand.

After the workshop to discuss brand strategy, it is highly advisable to produce a contact report detailing the responses, findings and views. This should be signed off and approved by the management team before the creative brand team begins any conceptual work.

Brand identity concepts

The next stage for the team is the conceptual stage, which will result in the presentation of the brand identity elements: brand name, strapline, logo, mascot (if relevant), colour, typography and aesthetics. If a name and strapline are to be decided, it will be necessary to approve these before committing to the visual treatment of these primary elements.

The creative brand team will typically prepare up to three conceptual approaches for the brand identity, visualized across an appropriate range of materials, for example business stationery, advertising and the website. The team will need to convince the management team that their concepts can be practically executed, as the management team may be inexperienced at imagining how the ideas will be applied. The presented material may extend to signage, vehicle livery, packaging, merchandise and uniforms.

The chosen concept may require development before it reaches final approval. When the concept is signed off, final digital artwork will be created and guidelines explaining how to use the basic brand identity elements will be produced.

The brand identity will provide a system for all communications and expressions of the brand at each touchpoint.

In the final chapter we will look at sustaining and protecting the valuable brand you have created.

Summary

An investment in design can transform the fortunes of brands and contribute to the economies of nations, as witnessed by the transformation of the Samsung brand in South Korea. Design is a critical differentiator that distinguishes brands from their market competitors.

The spirit of creativity and the courage to seek answers to questions drive innovation and open doors to new markets. A long-term commitment to design and innovation is essential for the continued success of the brand.

SUNDAY
MONDAY
TUESDAY
WEDNESDAY
THURSDAY
FRIDAY
SATURDAY

Fact-check [Answers at the back]

1. Raymond Loewy is recognized as the father of which type of design?
   a) Graphic design ❑
   b) Product design ❑
   c) Fashion design ❑
   d) Industrial design ❑

2. Which artistic movement is the designer William Morris associated with?
   a) The Bauhaus ❑
   b) De Stijl ❑
   c) Arts and Crafts ❑
   d) Art Deco ❑

3. How did the designer Thomas Heatherwick contribute to the London 2012 Olympic Games?
   a) Olympic Stadium design ❑
   b) London 2012 logo design ❑
   c) The Cauldron design ❑
   d) A bicycle design ❑

4. Which brand is Sir Jonathan Ive closely associated with?
   a) Samsung ❑
   b) Braun ❑
   c) HTC ❑
   d) Apple ❑

5. What is the 'symbolic value' of an object according to French philosopher Jean Baudrillard?
   a) Basic purpose ❑
   b) Economic value ❑
   c) Sentimental value ❑
   d) Significant value relative to a measure of quality ❑

6. What is the essence of 'good design' according to the German industrial designer Dieter Rams?
   a) Less but better ❑
   b) Less is more ❑
   c) More or less ❑
   d) Minimalism ❑

7. Samsung's brand revolution began with an executive meeting in which city?
   a) Cologne ❑
   b) Frankfurt ❑
   c) Dusseldorf ❑
   d) Berlin ❑

8. Fashion designer Christopher Bailey is associated with the success of which brand?
   a) Mulberry ❑
   b) Burberry ❑
   c) Blackberry ❑
   d) Barbour ❑

9. Jock Kinneir and Margaret Calvert are famous for which UK information design system?
   a) The Festival of Britain ❑
   b) Heathrow Airport Terminal 5 ❑
   c) Road signs ❑
   d) London 2012 Olympic Games ❑

10. Who designed the London Underground map?
   a) Neville Brody ❑
   b) Abram Games ❑
   c) Alfred Leete ❑
   d) Harry Beck ❑

SATURDAY

Sustaining the brand

The fast-paced change of social media has provided opportunities and threats to brands, making it easier for consumers to celebrate and criticize the products and services they use. Brands are forced to be more transparent than ever before in the digital era.

As brands grow and gain market share, they become attractive to counterfeiters and imitators eager to cut corners and jump on the success bandwagon. The careful management of the brand includes the protection of its intellectual property. If you don't take your brand's assets seriously, they will be vulnerable to copycats and opportunists.

The successful implementation of any brand identity programme requires digital artwork files and guidelines. When outside agencies are engaged to produce marketing and promotional items, they will require adequate resources and guidance.

Brand touchpoints

Ludwig Mies van der Rohe is credited with coining the phrase 'God is in the detail.' The celebrated German architect believed that whatever we do, we should do thoroughly, and this is certainly true for brands. Touchpoints are the chain of interactions that collectively form the customer experience. Each touchpoint tests the brand promise and that promise is only as strong as its weakest link.

Touchpoints thus have a critical role in delivering a rewarding customer experience. Each customer experience is a procession of details. These details are the brand's touchpoints and the analysis and improvement of their delivery can return significant gains.

Customers, employees and suppliers will experience multiple touchpoints during their relationship with the brand. A mutually satisfying outcome at each touchpoint strengthens the brand relationship and lays a path to loyalty.

These interactions all have the potential to add value to the customer relationship by making them rewarding and unique to the brand. It is important to identify which interactions add the greatest significance to the customer's loyalty and ensure that these touchpoints are protected and carefully managed.

The evaluation of touchpoints can reveal weaknesses in the relationship and provide opportunities to improve the brand experience. Powerful brands ensure that the brand experience is always in keeping with the brand's values and ethos. Observing and cataloguing the customer experience step by step makes it possible to identify stress points before they break and damage consumer relationships. Some touchpoints will add more value to the customer experience than others and they should be rated and prioritized according to significance.

Guests at expensive hotels would notice the absence of bathroom luxuries like soaps, shampoos and scents because the inclusion of these details is an indicator that the customer is valued. If the details meet expectations, the overall customer experience will be fulfilled; compromising on an important detail can have a detrimental impact on everything else.

The careful mapping of each stage in the customer experience can reveal insights and opportunities for change and innovation. In order to judge the effectiveness of each interaction, the touchpoint should be evaluated on a scale from 1 to 5 for effectiveness.

 TIP *The process of monitoring touchpoints can lead to innovation, and the commitment to continuous improvement should create new levels of service value. Viewing the bigger picture enables the brand manager to see new connections.*

The customer loyalty journey

The customer loyalty journey provides a method for appraising customer satisfaction. It makes it possible to monitor which sections of the route are effective at engaging customers and which points of the journey need improvement to avoid losing business.

Brand touchpoints may be categorized into three broad areas according to the point the customer has reached in their relationship with the brand:

● awareness
● commitment
● loyalty.

'Awareness' touchpoints

This is the pre-purchase phase of the customer relationship and concerns the touchpoints before purchase. Potential brand converts will learn about the brand through a variety of means including personal referral, advertising, email, website, social media and marketing material. These touchpoints are directed at audience awareness. Existing customers will also be affected by the quality of these touchpoints.

Pre-purchase touchpoints serve to inform the customer audience why this brand is better than any other on the market and how it is relevant to their life.

'Commitment' touchpoints

This is the purchase phase of the journey. The customer has raised their awareness of the brand and is now committed to an investment in the brand.

These touchpoints are personal interactions with the brand that include point of sale, employee behaviour, packaging, product design and online performance. This critical phase must confirm the audience's choice in making the right decision.

'Loyalty' touchpoints

The 'loyalty' touchpoints are in the post-purchase phase of the journey. The customer has purchased the brand and put it to the test. The outcome of the brand performance will affect the likelihood of them buying again or referring the brand to their family and social circle.

These touchpoints concern the continued performance of the brand and its ability to fulfil the customer's expectations and may include customer support, instructions, help desk, follow-up communications via telephone, post and email, the overall performance and the longevity of the brand.

Social media

It's often said that 'a brand is not what you [the brand owner] say it is, it's what they [the consumers] say it is' and social media give consumers a very loud voice to share exactly what's on their mind. Since Twitter began in 2006, the microblogging social media site has attracted over 645 million registered users (by January 2014) and, according to statisticbrain.com, more than 135,000 new users are signing up each day. Celebrities and politicians from Justin Bieber to Barack Obama command the biggest audiences and have a considerable influence in shaping the opinions of their followers.

Consumers are more likely to act on personal referrals from trusted sources than blindly accept the words of advertisers. They are now talking directly to other consumers and the dialogue is beyond the control of brand managers. Brands can no longer monopolize the dialogue.

Brand casting

The seemingly endless opportunities presented through social media make it possible for brands to broadcast using video and audio. Brands can join in and feed the buzz about them through branded Facebook pages, Twitter accounts, Blogs, Pinterest and YouTube channels, for example. Social media represent an important tool for keeping the conversation about your brand flowing.

Considerations for social media

It is essential that the personality of the brand remains consistent in every area of branded communication. The online brand strategy should integrate seamlessly with the audience's experience in the physical world. The tone of voice, use of language and imagery should be consistent in both online and offline communication.

The success of 'apps' on smartphones and tablet devices puts the power of social media in the palm of the consumer's hand. Reading a Twitter timeline or checking your latest posts on Instagram places greater emphasis on the use of quality photography when uploading pictorial content to your account and for the user profile. It's worth considering how effective your chosen profile image will appear when reduced to a very small icon on a timeline. It's increasingly common for LinkedIn users to take their personal branding seriously and invest in professionally taken portraits for their accounts. Photography and copywriting skills come to the fore in building a consistent style. Choice of words and snappy headlines grab the attention and compel the audience to take notice and read further.

Anyone given responsibility for producing online content must be aware of his or her duty of care to the brand. With the ease and simplicity of social media communication, users must not forget that they are publishing and are bound by the laws of libel. High-profile celebrity 'personality brands' are discovering to their cost the price of making ill-considered comments online.

It is easy to be seduced by the power and instant access of services like Facebook, Twitter, LinkedIn and YouTube, but it is essential not to lose sight of the brand and to maintain a consistent tone of voice and personality throughout all communication. Without a clear strategy for posting online content, poorly written messages, ill-considered pictures and irrelevant videos can do great harm to the reputation of the brand.

Protecting your asset

Imitation may be the sincerest form of flattery but it's no compliment when a competitor emulates your brand or, worse still, copies it directly. Hijacking a competitor's brand by using similar brand aesthetics to confuse or manipulate the consumer is nothing new. Supermarkets often push boundaries and get dangerously close to matching well-known brand names with their own-brand in-house packaging. Consumers are willing to spend more on strong brands because they believe in their authenticity.

When a new idea gains momentum and takes a significant share of the market, it inevitably becomes attractive to the 'me too' type of competitor, bereft of his or her own ideas and eager to exploit the equity of the leading brand. You can't stop competition, but brands can protect their intellectual property (IP) and build stronger emotional barriers to competition through their culture and personality.

Advantages of intellectual property

● Careful stewardship of your IP creates a stronger barrier to competition and a level of protection against counterfeiters and imitators.
● Brand owners who carefully manage their IP realize a higher price for their brand when selling the business.
● Brands can be licensed or franchised, when the intellectual property rights are managed.

Licensing

When a brand really stands for something, it becomes attractive to other brands that are eager to borrow some of the successful brand's value to sell their own products and services. Obvious examples of this are when Hollywood studios license characters and movie branding for use on lunch boxes and T-shirts. This strategy is financially profitable for the brand owner and increases the brand's exposure to a wider market. Types of licence include copyright, merchandising, patent and trademark.

Considerations for licensing

It is essential that the licensed product or service reflects the values and qualities associated with the brand. Licensing a brand to mismatched products or inferior-quality merchandise will affect the customer's perception of the brand and may be detrimental in the long term.

Franchising

If you have a successful branded business model, it may be attractive to grow the brand through franchising. The franchisor sells the rights of their business model to an entrepreneur (the franchisee). The franchisee buys the rights to use the proven branded format for a fixed period of time in an agreed territory or location.

Themed restaurants are perfect business models for franchising. Famous examples of franchises include McDonald's, Subway, Pizza Hut and 7-Eleven.

Considerations for franchising

It is important that the franchisor carefully selects their franchisees for values and culture. The behaviour and performance of the franchisee will affect consumers' perceptions of the brand and will inform their expectations of other franchisees.

Start by protecting your name

If you are considering a new brand name it's advisable to check its legal availability before getting too attached to your choice. If the brand is also the company name, it will be necessary to check with the government requirements for your region. In the UK, limited companies are registered at Companies House.

An online presence is practically mandatory, so it is important to check the availability of matching Internet domain names for your website and usernames for social media accounts. If the preferred choice of name is already taken, a variation or creative solution may be required, but be careful not to make it too difficult for customers to find online or remember.

SUNDAY

MONDAY

TUESDAY

WEDNESDAY

THURSDAY

FRIDAY

SATURDAY

TIP *Some straightforward checks you can do yourself that will save time and expense are:*

- *domain name check*
- *social media check*
- *limited company check.*

Categories of intellectual property

The four main categories of intellectual property are:

- trademarks
- copyright
- design rights
- patents.

Trademarks

You can trademark unique distinctive words, logos, slogans and designs that identify branded goods and services. Successful registration qualifies the owner to display the ® symbol to indicate that it cannot be used by anyone else and is enforced by law.

Copyright

Copyright protects literature, drama, music, art, broadcasting, sound recordings and film. It is the automatic right of the originator and does not require application. To indicate copyright ownership, the originator simply needs to display their authorship in proximity to the protected work, for example Copyright © Author name 2014.

Design rights

Design rights apply to the shape and the visual look of an object. All original designs are automatically protected for a fixed period of time and a registered design will increase the protection.

Patents

Patents protect the processes and features that make things work. Inventors profit from their inventions by patenting their ideas. Successful application for a patent means that no one will be legally permitted to make, use, import or sell the invention without the permission of the patent holder.

Considerations for intellectual property (IP)

Appoint an intellectual property lawyer to advise on your intellectual property assets. There are a variety of specific levels of brand protection available including confidentiality agreements, database rights, protection abroad and trade secrets. Refer to the Intellectual Property Authority for your region. It is important that you are properly protected in order to safeguard the future of your brand.

Maintaining standards

The traditional method of spreading the brand idea was through giant books of rules and examples, kept under the watchful eye of the brand guardian. These reference books were largely the preserve of the marketing department. The accessibility of digital media and the immediacy of the Internet made the distribution of brand guidelines and artwork much easier to manage. However you share the information, the most important thing is to make it accessible.

Brand books and brand identity guidelines

The 'brand book', regardless of its physical format, needs to be an inspiring manifesto for the purpose of breathing life into the brand idea. The 'brand identity guidelines' are the reference manual for implementing the brand.

Considerations for the brand books

- **Format:** Website, PDF, magazine, newsletter or appropriate medium to catch the attention of its target audience.
- **Tone of voice:** Keep it motivating, engaging and appropriate to the brand personality and excite the audience to the brand's potential.

- **Audience:** The brand book is aimed at all employees to raise awareness of employee behaviour and create ambassadors for the brand.
- **Brand strategy:** Explain the key brand criteria: purpose, vision, values, mission statement, proposition, positioning, personality and audience. Imagine that you are explaining the idea to someone who does not speak the same language. Keep it simple and illustrate with examples. The document should open with a letter of endorsement from the brand champion.

Suggested contents for the brand identity guidelines

1 Message of endorsement from CEO/brand champion
2 Brand guardians and contact details
3 The brand strategy – key brand criteria
4 Brand architecture
5 The brand identity basic elements – name, strapline, logo, mascot, colour, type, aesthetics
6 Digital artwork
7 Stationery and templates
8 Literature styles – brochures, leaflets, etc.
9 Typographic grids and templates
10 Packaging
11 Digital media – email, website
12 Social media – Twitter, Facebook, LinkedIn, YouTube, Pinterest, Instagram, etc.
13 Presentations – proposals and Microsoft PowerPoint templates
14 Advertising – print, web, mobile devices, TV, outdoor
15 Exhibitions – trade shows, pop-up stands, banners
16 Wayfinding/Signage – internal and external
17 Vehicle livery
18 Uniforms
19 Merchandise – T-shirts, caps, badges, pens, etc.

Considerations for the brand identity guidelines

- **Format:** Website, PDF or appropriate medium for access by staff with a responsibility to create branded communications.

- **Purpose:** The brand identity guidelines explain the basic elements of the brand identity and how to use them to create consistent branded communication.
- **Responsibility:** Appoint someone as the brand guardian with stewardship for the day-to-day protection of the brand and its correct implementation, both internally (for employee communications) and externally (for customers). This role typically falls under the marketing department. The document should open with a letter of endorsement from the brand champion and a firm reminder that there will be penalties if the brand identity guidelines are not followed.

Digital artwork

There is an array of digital file formats available for specific uses including EPS, PDF, JPEG, GIF, TIFF, PNG, BMP and WMF. It is advisable that these are created by graphics professionals and tested for reproduction before they are made available. Guidelines for the files' correct application should be made available together with the artwork. These master artwork files must never be changed, customized, adapted or distorted. They exist for the single purpose of maintaining the brand's consistent appearance.

The files should only be issued to trusted parties. They have great value because they authenticate the items they appear on, so take care and note who they are shared with.

Summary

Touchpoints are the individual events in a sequence that deliver the overall brand experience. These details occur in every department within an organization and the big challenge is to deliver brand consistency across every facet of the enterprise.

The fast-growing area of social media provides exciting opportunities for the future growth of brands. Employees with responsibility for publishing content online have a special duty of care to the brand's reputation.

Brand owners need to take precautions to protect their intellectual property so that they may realize the full value of their investment. Licensing and franchising can offer profitable revenue options for the fully protected brand owner.

A brand book and set of guidelines are essential tools for sharing the brand idea and to signify to all audiences, both internal and external, that you care about this brand and their contribution.

SUNDAY

MONDAY

TUESDAY

WEDNESDAY

THURSDAY

FRIDAY

SATURDAY

Fact-check [Answers at the back]

1. What is a brand touchpoint?
a) A conversation with sales staff ❑
b) A purchase via an online retailer ❑
c) An advert in a newspaper ❑
d) All of the above ❑

2. What famous phrase is attributed to the architect Ludwig Mies van der Rohe?
a) The medium is the message ❑
b) Any colour – so long as it's black ❑
c) God is in the detail ❑
d) Genius is 1 per cent inspiration, 99 per cent perspiration ❑

3. What is the advantage of touchpoint mapping?
a) To identify stress points in the customer experience ❑
b) Risk assessment ❑
c) To gain insights that lead to innovation ❑
d) All of the above ❑

4. Which social media service caught the headlines when the high-street retailer HMV made rapid redundancies in January 2013?
a) Facebook ❑
b) LinkedIn ❑
c) Twitter ❑
d) Instagram ❑

5. Which of these high-street brands is a franchise model?
a) Aldi ❑
b) McDonald's ❑
c) Tiger ❑
d) John Lewis ❑

6. How many new users signed up to Twitter each day in January 2014?
a) 1,300 ❑
b) 135,000 ❑
c) 13,500 ❑
d) 5,000 ❑

7. What does copyright protect?
a) The shape and visual look of an object ❑
b) The processes and features that make things work ❑
c) Literature, drama, music, art, broadcasting, sound recordings and film ❑
d) Unique distinctive words or slogans ❑

8. What are design rights?
a) A consumer organization ❑
b) Special privileges for designers ❑
c) A code of ethics for designers ❑
d) The automatic legal protection of original designs ❑

9. What is the best strategy to protect your intellectual property?
a) Do it yourself ❑
b) Seek professional legal advice ❑
c) Appoint a member of staff ❑
d) Leave it to chance ❑

10. Who is responsible for brand guidelines?
a) The brand champion ❑
b) The brand ambassador ❑
c) The brand guardian ❑
d) The brand advocate ❑

Further reading

Aaker, David A., *Building Strong Brands* (Pocket Books, 2010).

Cooper, Rachel & Press, Mike, *The Design Agenda: A Guide to Successful Design Management* (John Wiley & Sons, 1995).

de Chernatony, Leslie, *From Brand Vision to Brand Evaluation* (Routledge, 2010).

Godin, Seth, *Purple Cow: Transform your business by being remarkable* (Penguin Books, 2005).

Hitchens, Julia & Hitchens, Paul, *Create the Perfect Brand: Teach Yourself* (Hodder Education, 2010).

Holloman, Christer, *The Social Media MBA: Your Competitive Edge in Social Media Strategy Development and Delivery* (John Wiley & Sons, 2012).

Keller, Kevin Lane, Apéria, Tony & Georgson, Mats, *Strategic Brand Management – A European Perspective* (FT Prentice Hall, 2011).

Lindstrom, Martin, *Brand Sense: Sensory secrets behind the stuff we buy* (Kogan Page, 2010).

Mark, Margaret & Pearson, Carol S.,*The Hero and the Outlaw: Building extraordinary brands through the power of archetypes* (McGraw-Hill, 2001).

Mollerup, Per, *Marks of Excellence: The History and Taxonomy of Trademarks* (Phaidon Press Limited, 2013).

Neumeier, Marty, *Zag: The number one strategy for high-performance brands* (New Riders, 2006).

Olins, Wally, *The Brand Handbook* (Thames & Hudson, 2008).

Rhoades, Ann, *Built on Values* (Jossey-Bass (a Wiley imprint), 2011).

Ries, Al & Ries, Laura, *The 22 Immutable Laws of Branding* (Profile Books, 2000).

Sartain, Libby & Schumann, Mark, *Brand from the inside: Eight essentials to emotionally connect your employees to your business* (Jossey-Bass (a Wiley imprint), 2006).

Wheeler, Alina, *Designing Brand Identity: an essential guide for the whole branding team* (John Wiley & Sons, 2012).

Surviving in tough times

In tough times and at the onset of economic recession, the first impulse for many businesses is to cap spending. Despite the advice of seasoned businesspeople to market your way out of a recession, marketing budgets are usually the first to go. It may seem counter-intuitive, but a recession can prove to be the best time to build a brand and there are prime examples of household brands that began in difficult times, including General Electric (1890), Walt Disney (1923), Burger King (1953) and Microsoft (1975).

What are the winning qualities for surviving a recession? How do you emerge with your brand in good health? What are the strategies used by some of the hardiest brands in times of recession?

1 Think differently

Doing things differently can create rewarding and memorable experiences. Branding makes it clear to the consumer why a product is better than any other on offer. Celebrate the difference that makes you stand apart from your market competitors. Clarity and focus are vital – be clear about what makes you special and what it means to your customers.

2 Back a champion

The founder, owner or CEO must be ready at all times to promote the brand in any situation and set an excellent example to employees and key stakeholders. A confident and strong brand champion inspires team morale and improves investor relations.

3 Appoint ambassadors

Each member of staff in an organization is a brand ambassador, and it's important they understand the part they play in building its success. Invest in people – a positive spirit of fellowship and common purpose among employees is essential for brand confidence.

4 Make the world a better place

Every organization, product or service must have a 'reason for being', so identify what your brand does and the benefit it provides, making sure it's clear and easy to understand. Is your brand relevant to current market conditions? Are you offering value, convenience or well-being? In a recession, consumers will take great care in how they spend their money.

5 Look to the future

Every organization must innovate to survive and can't afford to stagnate by expecting their customers to keep buying the same products. Sometimes we simply can't imagine what we want until we see it. Create demand – give people what they didn't know they needed but cannot imagine ever having lived without, with new products, services and brands.

6 Know what you believe in

A brand's values are what it stands for and what it believes in; they're the guidelines that form the organization's moral compass. If you hire expensive celebrities or famous talent to champion your brand, you must be careful to monitor their behaviour so that it doesn't compromise your brand's values.

7 Make what you do count

Consumers can see past glitzy marketing campaigns and seductive advertising. As the old adage goes, the proof of the pudding is in the eating and actions will always speak louder than words.

8 Offer great value

Great value for money doesn't just mean offering the cheapest price. A brand can offer value above and beyond the price label by granting the customer the satisfaction of owning a leading brand. Every organization can focus on its quality and service levels to offer a higher level of care and durability. A recession affects consumer confidence. A proven track record will pay dividends. New enterprises will need to work hard for credibility. Do what you say and be consistent – loyalty is born of trust.

9 Get to the front of the queue

In a crowded marketplace, it's difficult to stand out if you're the seventh best-selling brand. The opportunity is to identify the attributes that differentiate your product and promote your brand as the leader in that category. Positioning places the brand at the front of the queue for the consumer's attention. A recession can clear out a lot of the market competition and leave the strongest and leanest brands in pole position for success.

10 Do community service

By recognizing the groups that interact with a brand, you build up a picture of an interdependent community, which includes employees, suppliers, investors, banks, government and customers. This community is never passive; it's an interactive entity with an interest in the brand. The interest these groups have in the brand extends beyond the buyer–seller relationship. The success of social media has created a platform for valuable consumer interaction.

Thank you!

Successful brand management requires energy, enthusiasm and dynamism. The universal goal must be to deliver the best brand experience possible, guided by a shared feeling for what the brand is and stands for.

As the late Steve Jobs said, 'Have the courage to follow your heart and intuition. They somehow already know what you truly want to become. Everything else is secondary.'

We wish you every success with your brand.

Answers

Sunday: 1d; 2b; 3b; 4c; 5d; 6b; 7b; 8d; 9a; 10b.

Monday: 1d; 2a; 3b; 4d; 5c; 6a; 7d; 8b; 9c; 10d.

Tuesday: 1c; 2c; 3b; 4b; 5b; 6a; 7b; 8d; 9b; 10a.

Wednesday: 1c; 2c; 3b; 4b; 5a; 6b; 7c; 8a; 9c; 10d.

Thursday: 1d; 2c; 3d; 4c; 5a; 6a; 7c; 8b; 9c; 10a.

Friday: 1d; 2c; 3c; 4d; 5c; 6a; 7b; 8b; 9c; 10d.

Saturday: 1d; 2c; 3d; 4c; 5b; 6b; 7c; 8d; 9b; 10c.